Rick Steves®

POCKET

BARCELONA

Rick Steves with Gene Openshaw
and Cameron Hewitt

Contents

Introduction 3

The Ramblas Ramble .15

Barri Gòtic Walk 35

Cathedral of Barcelona Tour 53

Picasso Museum Tour 63

Eixample Walk 77

Sagrada Família Tour 93

Sights 107

Sleeping 135

Eating 143

Practicalities 159

Index 183

Introduction

As Spain's second city and the capital of the Catalan people, Barcelona bubbles with life. It's a city of distinct neighborhoods, from the tangled lanes of the Barri Gòtic to the trendy boulevards of the Eixample. It has its own unmistakable "look"—ironwork balconies, flower boxes, sidewalk mosaics, and the fanciful curves of Modernista masters like Antoni Gaudí. There's groundbreaking art from Barcelona's own Pablo Picasso and Joan Miró. The cafés are filled by day, and people crowd the streets at night, popping into tapas bars for a drink and a perfectly composed bite of seafood.

Simply put, Barcelona is unique, with a language, history, and culture separate from the rest of Spain and found nowhere else. If you're in the mood to surrender to a city's charms, let it be Barcelona.

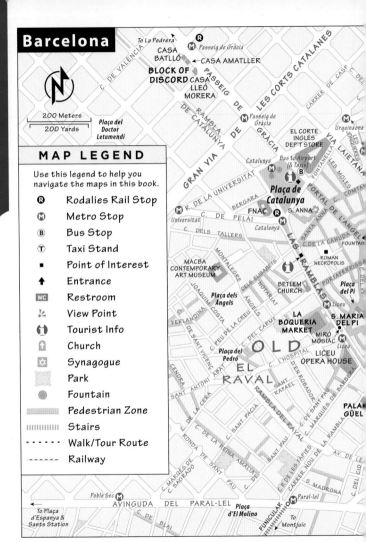

Barcelona

To La Pedrera

CASA BATLLÓ

CASA AMATLLER

BLOCK OF DISCORD

CASA LLEÓ MORERA

200 Meters

200 Yards

Plaça del Doctor Letamendi

MAP LEGEND

Use this legend to help you navigate the maps in this book.

Ⓡ	Rodalies Rail Stop
Ⓜ	Metro Stop
Ⓑ	Bus Stop
Ⓣ	Taxi Stand
▪	Point of Interest
♦	Entrance
WC	Restroom
⅄	View Point
ⓘ	Tourist Info
⛪	Church
✡	Synagogue
▓	Park
●	Fountain
▨▨▨	Pedestrian Zone
▥▥▥	Stairs
· · · · ·	Walk/Tour Route
- - - - -	Railway

Passeig de Gràcia

PASSEIG DE GRÀCIA

C. DE VALÈNCIA

LES CORTS CATALANES

CARRER DE CASP

RAMBLA DE CATALUNYA

GRAN VIA

Passeig de Gràcia

EL CORTE INGLÉS DEP'T STORE

Urquinaona

VIA LAIETANA

FONTANELLA

Catalunya

Bus to Airport (& Taxis)

Plaça de Catalunya

R. DE LA UNIVERSITAT

BERGARA

PORTAL DE L'ANGEL

PORTAL DE L'ANGEL

COMTA

FNAC Ⓡ S. ANNA

Universitat

C. DE PELAI

Catalunya

SANTA ANNA

C. DELS TALLERS

C. DE LA CANUDA

FOUNTAIN

MONTALEGRE

C. DELS ELISABETS

MACBA CONTEMPORARY ART MUSEUM

ROMAN NECROPOLIS

LAS RAMBLAS

ANGELS

BETLEM CHURCH

Plaça dels Àngels

Plaça del Pi

PORTAFERRISSA

JOAQUIM COSTA

C. NOTARIAT

Liceu

FERLANDINA

DE SANT VICENÇ

C. DEL CARME

PEU DE LA CREU

LA BOQUERIA MARKET

S. MARIA DEL PI

MIRÓ MOSAIC

Plaça del Pedró

L'HOSPITAL

Liceu

LICEU OPERA HOUSE

OLD

EL RAVAL

SANT RAFAEL

D'EN ROBADOR

RAMBLA DEL RAVAL

C. DE SANT PAU

MARQUES DE BARBERÀ

CENDRA

SANT ANTONI ABAT

C. DE LA CERA

SANT PACIÀ

PALAU GÜEL

C. MARQUÉS DEL DUERO

C. DE LES TÀPIES

CARRER NOU DE LA RAMBLA

AV. DE LE

C. DE

CID

RONDA DE LA REINA AMÀLIA

C. DE LA REINA AMÀLIA

C. MARQUÈS DE SANT PAU

C. SAGRADO

S. MADRONA

Poble Sec

FUNICULAR

Paral·lel

To Plaça d'Espanya & Sants Station

AVINGUDA DEL PARAL·LEL

C. DE BLAI

Plaça d'El Molino

To Montjuïc

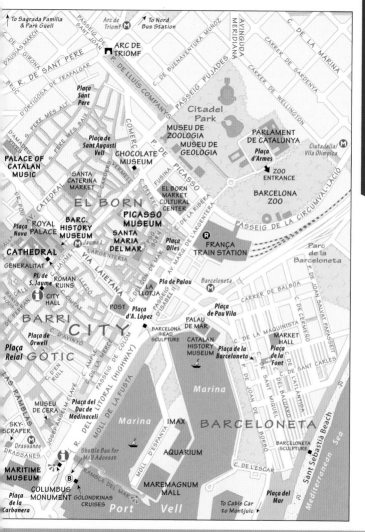

↑ To Sagrada Familia & Park Güell

Arc de Triomf Ⓜ

↑ To Nord Bus Station

ARC DE TRIOMF

PASSEIG DE SANT JOAN

C. DE LLUIS COMPANYS

AVINGUDA MERIDIANA

C. DE LA MARINA

CARRER DE SARDENYA

CARRER DE WELLINGTON

C. DE BUENAVENTURA MUÑOZ

Plaça Sant Pere

D'AUSIAS MARCH

R. DE SANT PERE

GIRONA DE

D'ORTIGOSA DE TRAFALGAR

BRUC

S. PERE MÉS ALT

D'AMADEU VIVES

S. PERE MÉS BAX

PERE MÉS BAIX

COMERÇ

P. DE LLUIS COMPANYS

PASSEIG PUJADES

Citadel Park

MUSEU DE ZOOLOGIA

MUSEU DE GEOLOGIA

PARLAMENT DE CATALUNYA

Plaça d'Armes

Ciutadella/ Vila Olimpica Ⓜ

ZOO ENTRANCE

BARCELONA ZOO

PALACE OF CATALAN MUSIC

Plaça de Sant Augusti Vell

CHOCOLATE MUSEUM

SANTA CATERINA MARKET

CARDERS

P. DEL REC

FUSINA

PICASSO

EL BORN MARKET CULTURAL CENTER

AV. MARQ. DE L'ARGENTERA

PASSEIG DE LA CIRCUMVAL·LACIÓ

CAPUTXES

EL BORN

ROYAL PALACE

BARC. HISTORY MUSEUM

PICASSO MUSEUM

SANTA MARIA DEL MAR

Plaça Olles

FRANÇA TRAIN STATION

Plaça Nova

CATEDRAL

Plaça de Sant Miquel

Ⓜ Jaume I

VIA LAIETANA

L'ARGENTERIA

Parc de la Barceloneta

CATHEDRAL

GENERALITAT

Pl. de S. Jaume

ROMAN RUINS

JAUME I

C. DEL CALL

LLEDÓ

DE LA CIUTAT

C. DELS CORDERS DE MAR

PASSEIG DEL BORN

C. D'ISABEL II

Pla de Palau

Barceloneta Ⓜ

CARRER DE BALBOA

P. DE JOAN SALVAT PAPASSEIT

ⓘ CITY HALL

POST

Plaça d'A. López

LA LLOTJA

Plaça de Pau Vila

DE CERMENO

BARRI

CITY

D'AVINYÓ

BARCELONA HEAD SCULPTURE

PALAU DE MAR

CATALAN HISTORY MUSEUM

Plaça de la Barceloneta

C. DE LA MAQUINISTA

MARKET HALL

Plaça de la Font

P. DE SANT CARLES

C. DE SANT MIGUEL

Plaça de Orwell

GÒTIC

Plaça Reial

C. D'EN RULL

C. D'EN GIGNÀS

C. AMPLE

C. DE LA MERCÈ

PASSEIG DE COLOM

R. DE LA LLOTJA

MOLL DE LA FUSTA

PASSEIG DEL LITORAL (HIGHWAY)

Marina

C. DE JOAN DE BORBÓ

C. DE L'ATLANTIDO

C. DEL BALUARD

BARCELONETA

LAS RAMBLAS

MUSEU DE CERA

Plaça del Duc de Medinaceli

Marina

IMAX

Mediterranean Sea

SKY-SCRAPER

Drassanes

DRASSANES

ⓘ

MOLL D'ESPANYA

AQUARIUM

C. DE L'ESCAR

BARCELONETA SCULPTURE

Sant Sebastià Beach

MARITIME MUSEUM

Shuttle Bus for Moll Adossat

Ⓑ

RAMBLA DEL MAR

MAREMAGNUM MALL

Plaça del Mar

COLUMBUS MONUMENT

GOLONDRINAS CRUISES

Plaça de la Carbonera

Port Vell

To Cable Car to Montjuïc ↓

About This Book

With this book, I've selected only the best of Barcelona—admittedly, a tough call. The core of the book is six self-guided walks and tours that zero in on Barcelona's greatest sights and neighborhoods.

My Ramblas Ramble introduces you to this lively city with a walk down one of Europe's great people-watching boulevards. The Barri Gòtic Walk and Cathedral of Barcelona Tour lay the historical ground-work for your exploration of the area's atmospheric lanes and courtyards. At the Picasso Museum, you can see how the artist's formative years in Barcelona shaped his illustrious career. The Eixample Walk focuses on the city's colorful legacy of Modernisme, while showing off the upscale side of Barcelona. Finally, there's the epic unfinished church begun by Gaudí—Sagrada Família, whose prickly spires have become a symbol of the city.

The rest of the book is a traveler's tool kit. You'll find plenty more about Barcelona's attractions, from shopping to nightlife to enjoying Barcelona's tapas bars. And there are helpful hints on saving money, avoiding crowds, getting around town, enjoying a great meal, and more.

Key to This Book

Sights are rated:

▲▲▲ **Don't miss**

▲▲ **Try hard to see**

▲ **Worthwhile if you can make it**

No rating **Worth knowing about**

Tourist information offices are abbreviated as **TI**, and bathrooms are **WCs**.

Like Europe, this book uses the **24-hour clock.** It's the same through 12:00 noon, then keep going: 13:00 (1:00 p.m.), 14:00 (2:00 p.m.), and so on.

For **opening times**, if a sight is listed as "May–Oct daily 9:00–16:00," it should be open from 9 a.m. until 4 p.m. from the first day of May until the last day of October (but expect exceptions).

For **updates** to this book, visit www.ricksteves.com/update.

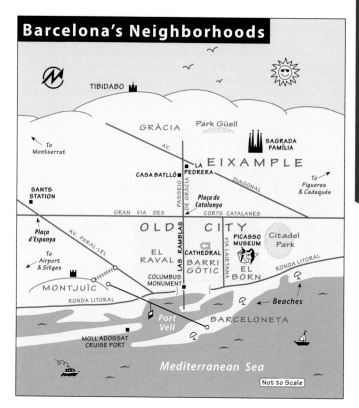

Barcelona's Neighborhoods

Barcelona by Neighborhood

The city of Barcelona slopes gently down a hillside to the sea. In the center sits Plaça de Catalunya, a large square that divides Barcelona into the Old City (south of the square) and new (north). Barcelona is huge and sprawling (1.6 million people), but—thanks to its walkable historic core and good public transit—all is manageable.

Think of Barcelona as a series of neighborhoods cradling major landmarks:

Plaça de Catalunya and the Ramblas: The huge, modern, central square—where all Catalunya gathers for major demonstrations—is home to big department stores, tourist services, public transportation, and convenient hotels. From here, the lively pedestrian drag called the Ramblas runs down to the harbor, past a colorful market, shops, restaurants, and street performers. To the west of the Ramblas lies the (unimportant-to-tourists) Raval neighborhood. To the east is the...

Barri Gòtic: With the cathedral as its navel, the Barri Gòtic (BAH-ree GOH-teek, Gothic Quarter) is the historic core of the Old City. It's a labyrinth of narrow streets that's ideal for strolling, shopping, dining on a pleasant square, and people-watching.

El Born: Farther east (across Via Laietana) is this rough-but-gentrifying district of shops, bistros, and nightlife, anchored by the Picasso Museum and Church of Santa Maria del Mar.

Harborfront: The old harbor, Port Vell, gleams with landmark monuments and new developments. Farther afield is the quaint neighborhood of Barceloneta (with great seafood restaurants) and a gorgeous man-made beach.

Eixample: Above Plaça de Catalunya, the elegant Eixample (eye-SHAM-plah) district has a grid street-plan of wide boulevards lined with chic tapas bars. Along its main axis, Passeig de Gràcia, are two Modernista highlights: the "Block of Discord" and La Pedrera.

Montjuïc: The large hill overlooking the harbor to the southwest is Montjuïc (mohn-jew-EEK). Its park-like setting is home to a panoramic castle, some excellent museums (Catalan Art, Joan Miró), and the Olympic Stadium. At the base of Montjuïc, stretching toward Plaça d'Espanya, is a complex of buildings, fountains, and vistas that showcase Barcelona today.

North of the Center: Beyond walking distance (but easily accessible by taxi, bus, or Metro) are Gaudí's Sagrada Família and Park Güell, the viewpoint hill of Tibidabo, and the artsy Gràcia district (north of Avenue Diagonal).

Cultural Orientation to Catalunya

Besides getting oriented geographically, it's wise to acquaint yourself with Barcelona's cultural landscape. Though part of Spain politically, the city and its region (Catalunya, or Cataluña) have a different language, heritage, and outlook.

All Barcelonans speak Spanish, but three-quarters prefer the local language, Catalan. If you know Spanish, by all means use it, but try to learn at least a handful of Catalan phrases: Please (*Si us plau;* see oos plow), thank you (*gracies,* GRAH-see-es), and more (⚫ see page 181).

Culturally, Catalunya is *not* the land of bullfighting, flamenco, and other Spanish clichés. It has its own calendar of local festivals, and its music, cuisine, and culture are more Mediterranean, European, and modern than they are traditionally Spanish.

Historically, Catalunya has run a parallel, independent course to the rest of Spain. Founded as a Roman retirement colony, it grew into a maritime power in the Middle Ages. These were its glory days, when the kingdom of Catalunya dominated the Mediterranean, and its unique culture was established. Then—when the rest of Spain discovered new trade routes to the Americas and entered its Golden Age—Catalunya declined. For centuries, it languished under the thumb of the central Spanish government in Madrid, which suppressed its language, government, and culture. In the 19th century, Catalunya had a rebirth (Renaixença), fueled by Industrial Age factories and creative geniuses like Gaudí who redesigned the city in Modernista style.

Today Catalunya cobbles together all these elements into a one-of-a-kind culture. On patriotic holidays, Catalunyans proudly take to the streets in the hundreds of thousands to demand greater autonomy from Madrid. You'll see Catalan symbolism in its red-and-gold-striped flag and images of the region's patron saint, the dragon-slaying St. George ("Jordi"). And citizens still gather in front of the cathedral to join hands and dance the local folk dance, the *sardana*.

Daily Reminder

Sunday: Most sights are open, but the Boqueria and Santa Caterina markets are closed. Some sights close early today, including the Fundació Joan Miró and Olympic and Sports Museum (which close at 14:30), along with the Chocolate Museum and Catalan Art Museum (which close at 15:00). Informal performances of the *sardana* national dance take place in front of the cathedral at noon (none in Aug). Some museums are free at certain times: Catalan Art Museum and Palau Güell (free on first Sun of month); Maritime Museum (free after 15:00); Picasso Museum, Barcelona History Museum, and Frederic Marès Museum (free on first Sun of month plus other Sun from 15:00). The Magic Fountains come alive on summer evenings (May-Sept).

Monday: Many sights are closed, including the Picasso Museum, Catalan Art Museum, Palau Güell, Barcelona History Museum, Casa Lleó Morera, *Santa Eulália* schooner (part of the Maritime Museum), Fundació Joan Miró, Frederic Marès Museum, Shoe Museum, El Born Cultural Center, and Olympic and Sports Museum. But most major Modernista sights are open today, including the Sagrada Família, La Pedrera, Park Güell, Casa Batlló, and Casa Amatller.

Planning Your Time

Barcelona is big, so plan your time carefully, carving up the metropolis into manageable sightseeing neighborhoods. These day plans give a sense of how much an energetic traveler can see in a few days:

Day 1: In the cool of the morning, follow my Barri Gòtic Walk and Cathedral of Barcelona Tour. Do my Ramblas Ramble, and then grab lunch in El Born or the Barri Gòtic. In the afternoon, tour the Palace of Catalan Music in El Born (advance reservation required). Trace my El Born walk, stopping off to do the Picasso Museum Tour. For dinner, either wait to dine at a restaurant when locals do (around 21:00) or bar-hop for tapas in El Born.

Tuesday: All major sights are open.

Wednesday: All major sights are open.

Thursday: All major sights are open. Fundació Joan Miró and the Picasso Museum are open until 21:30 year-round, and the Magic Fountains spout on summer evenings (May-Sept).

Friday: All major sights are open. The Magic Fountains light up Montjuïc year-round.

Saturday: All major sights are open. Barcelonans sometimes dance the *sardana* on Saturdays at 18:00 in front of the cathedral. The Magic Fountains dance all year. The Catalan Art Museum is free after 15:00.

Late-Hours Sightseeing: Sights with **year-round** evening hours (19:30 or later) include La Boqueria Market, the Maritime Museum, CaixaForum, Cathedral of Barcelona, Casa Batlló, Columbus Monument, Las Arenas, and the Church of Santa Maria del Mar. Sights offering later hours in **peak season** (roughly April-Sept) include the Sagrada Família, La Pedrera, Palau Güell, *Santa Eulàlia* schooner, Chocolate Museum, Park Güell, Fundació Joan Miró, Olympic and Sports Museum, Catalan Art Museum, Castle of Montjuïc, Spanish Village, Mies van der Rohe Pavilion, and the Gaudí House Museum.

Day 2: This is Modernisme Day. Start with my Eixample Walk, touring La Pedrera, Casa Lleó Morera (reservation required), and/or Casa Batlló. Eat an early lunch, and then take a taxi or bus to the Sagrada Família. In the later afternoon, visit either Park Güell or sights near the waterfront (Columbus Monument, mall, boat ride, Maritime Museum). In the evening, visit a sight that's open late (for a list, ✪ see above), take in a concert, or watch the illuminated Magic Fountains at Plaça de Espanya.

Day 3 and Beyond: Tour Montjuïc from top to bottom, stopping at the Catalan Art Museum, CaixaForum art gallery, and/or Fundació Joan Miró. If the weather is good, take the scenic cable-car ride from Montjuïc to the port, and spend the rest of the day at Barceloneta—stroll the promenade, hit the beach, and find your favorite *chiringuito* (beach bar) for dinner.

Barcelona at a Glance

▲▲▲**Ramblas** Barcelona's colorful, gritty, tourist-filled pedestrian thoroughfare. **Hours:** Always open. See page 15.

▲▲▲**Picasso Museum** Extensive collection offering insight into the brilliant Spanish artist's early years. **Hours:** Tue-Sun 9:00-19:00, Thu until 21:30, closed Mon. See page 63.

▲▲▲**Sagrada Família** Gaudí's remarkable, unfinished church—a masterpiece in progress. **Hours:** Daily April-Sept 9:00-20:00, Oct-March 9:00-18:00. See page 93.

▲▲**Palace of Catalan Music** Best Modernista interior in Barcelona. **Hours:** Fifty-minute English tours daily every hour 10:00-15:00, plus frequent concerts. See page 117.

▲▲**La Pedrera (Casa Milà)** Barcelona's quintessential Modernista building and Gaudí creation. **Hours:** Daily March-Oct 9:00-20:00, Nov-Feb 9:00-18:30. See page 122.

▲▲**Park Güell** Colorful Gaudí-designed park overlooking the city. **Hours:** Daily April-Oct 8:00-20:00 (May-Aug until 21:30), Nov-March 8:30-18:15. See page 123.

▲▲**Catalan Art Museum** World-class showcase of this region's art, including a substantial Romanesque collection. **Hours:** Tue-Sat 10:00-20:00 (Oct-April until 18:00), Sun 10:00-15:00, closed Mon. See page 130.

▲▲**CaixaForum** Modernista brick factory now occupied by cutting-edge cultural center featuring excellent temporary art exhibits. **Hours:** Daily 10:00-20:00. See page 132.

▲**La Boqueria Market** Colorful but touristy produce market, just off the Ramblas. **Hours:** Mon-Sat 8:00-20:00, best mornings after 9:00, closed Sun. See page 24.

▲**Palau Güell** Exquisitely curvy Gaudí interior and fantasy rooftop. **Hours:** Tue-Sun 10:00-20:00, Nov-March until 17:30, closed Mon. See page 110.

▲**Plaça Reial** Stately square near the Ramblas, with palm trees, Gaudí-designed lampposts, and a fine slice-of-life look at Barcelona. **Hours:** Always open. See page 29.

▲**Maritime Museum** A sailor's delight, housed in an impressive medieval shipyard (under renovation, so permanent collection not likely on display). **Hours:** Temporary exhibits daily 10:00-20:00. See page 111.

▲**Cathedral of Barcelona** Colossal Gothic cathedral ringed by distinctive chapels. **Hours:** Generally open to visitors Mon-Fri 8:00-19:30, Sat-Sun 8:00-20:00. See page 53.

▲*Sardana* **Dances** Patriotic dance in which proud Catalans join hands in a circle, often held outdoors. **Hours:** Every Sun at 12:00, sometimes also Sat at 18:00, no dances in Aug. See page 112.

▲**Barcelona History Museum** One-stop trip through town history, from Roman times to today. **Hours:** Tue-Sat 10:00-19:00, Sun 10:00-20:00, closed Mon. See page 114.

▲**Santa Caterina Market** Fine market hall built on the site of an old monastery and updated with a wavy Gaudí-inspired roof. **Hours:** Mon-Sat 7:30-15:30, Thu-Fri until 20:30, closed Sun. See page 117.

▲**Church of Santa Maria del Mar** Catalan Gothic church in El Born, built by wealthy medieval shippers. **Hours:** Generally open to visitors daily 9:00-20:30. See page 118.

▲**Casa Batlló** Gaudí-designed home topped with fanciful dragon-inspired roof. **Hours:** Daily 9:00-21:00. See page 120.

▲**Casa Lleó Morera** One of the best-preserved Modernista interiors in the city. **Hours:** Tour times vary, open Tue-Sun, closed Mon. See page 121.

▲**Fundació Joan Miró** World's best collection of works by Catalan modern artist Joan Miró and his contemporaries. **Hours:** Tue-Sat 10:00-20:00 (until 19:00 Oct-June), Thu until 21:00, Sun 10:00-14:30, closed Mon. See page 129.

▲**1929 World Expo Fairgrounds** Expo site at the base of Montjuïc, featuring playful Magic Fountains, impressive CaixaForum art gallery, and a faux Spanish Village. Las Arenas, a mall converted from a bull-ring, is nearby. **Hours:** Grounds always open. See page 131.

▲**Magic Fountains** Lively fountain spectacle. **Hours:** May-Sept Thu-Sun 21:00-23:00, Oct-April Fri-Sat 19:00-20:30. See page 131.

▲**Barcelona's Beaches** Fun-filled, man-made beaches with bike paths and trendy bars. **Hours:** Always open. See page 119.

If you have more days, there are several tempting day trips, including the mountaintop monastery of Montserrat, the beach resort town of Sitges, and the Salvador Dalí sights at Figueres and Cadaqués (✪ see page 134).

These are busy day-plans, so be sure to schedule in slack time for shopping, laundry, people-watching, leisurely dinners, and recharging your touristic batteries. Slow down and be open to unexpected experiences and the hospitality of the Catalunyan people.

Quick Tips: Reservations are required at the Palace of Catalan Music and Casa Lleó Morera. Avoid lines at a few key sights (Picasso Museum, Sagrada Família, Casa Batlló, La Pedrera, Palau Güell, and Park Güell's Monumental Zone) by buying advance tickets or a sightseeing pass (✪ see page 170 for details). Learn to navigate Barcelona by Metro, taxi, or bus (including the hop-on, hop-off Tourist Bus). Adapt to the Spanish eating schedule (late lunch, late dinner) or fill the gap with tapas. Barcelona stays up late, so consider an afternoon siesta to maximize energy for after dark.

Finally, remember that Barcelona itself is a great sight. Make time to wander, shop, and simply be.

I hope you have a great trip! Traveling like a temporary local and taking advantage of the information here, you'll enjoy the absolute most out of every mile, minute, and euro. I'm happy that you'll be visiting places I know and love, and meeting some of my favorite Spanish/Catalunyan people.

Happy travels! *Buen viaje!*

The Ramblas Ramble

From Plaça de Catalunya to the Waterfront

For more than a century, this walk down Barcelona's main boulevard has drawn locals and visitors alike. While its former elegance has been tacki-fied somewhat by tourist shops and fast-food joints, this promenade still has the best people-watching in town. Walk the Ramblas at least once to get the lay of the land, then venture farther afield. It's a one-hour, level stroll, with an easy return by Metro.

On this pedestrian-only Champs-Elysées, you'll raft the river of Barcelonese life, passing a grand opera house, elegant cafés, flower stands, retread prostitutes, brazen pickpockets, power-dressing con men, artists, street mimes, and people looking to charge more for a shoeshine than what you paid for the shoes.

ORIENTATION

Length of This Walk: Allow at least an hour. With limited time, focus on the first stretch, from Plaça de Catalunya to Liceu.

When to Go: It's always lively. By day, you get the best of La Boqueria Market. At night, you have all of Barcelona on parade.

Getting There: The walk begins at Plaça de Catalunya, across the square from El Corte Inglés department store (Metro: Plaça de Catalunya).

La Boqueria Market: Free, Mon-Sat 8:00-20:00, best mornings after 9:00, closed Sun, Rambla 91, Metro: Liceu, tel. 933-192-584, www. boqueria.info.

Columbus Monument: Elevator-€4.50, daily 8:30-20:30, Plaça del Portal de la Pau, Metro: Drassanes, tel. 933-025-224.

Eating: Touristy places are the norm here, but ✪ see page 149 for recommendations.

The Ramblas: The word "Ramblas" is plural; the street is actually a succession of five separately named segments. But street signs and addresses treat it as a single long street—"La Rambla," singular.

La Boqueria Market on the Ramblas

Plaça de Catalunya, the Tourist Bus hub

THE WALK BEGINS

▶ *Start on Plaça de Catalunya, at the top of the Ramblas.*

❶ Plaça de Catalunya

Dotted with fountains, statues, and pigeons, and ringed by grand Art Deco buildings, this plaza is Barcelona's center. The square's stern, straight lines are a reaction to the curves of Modernisme (which predominates in the Eixample district, just above the square). Plaça de Catalunya is the hub for the Metro, bus, airport shuttle, and Tourist Bus. It's where Barcelona congregates to watch soccer matches on the big screen, to demonstrate, to celebrate, and to enjoy outdoor concerts and festivals. More than half of the eight million Catalans live in greater Barcelona, and for the inhabitants of this proud nation, this is their Times Square.

Geographically and historically, the 12-acre square links the narrow streets of old Barcelona with the broad boulevards of the newer city. In the 1850s, when Barcelona tore down its medieval walls to expand the city, this square on the edge of the walls was one of the first places to be developed.

Four great thoroughfares radiate from here. The Ramblas is the popular pedestrian promenade. Passeig de Gràcia has fashionable shops and cafés (and noisy traffic). Rambla de Catalunya is equally fashionable but cozier and more pedestrian-friendly. Avinguda del Portal de l'Angel (shopper-friendly and traffic-free) leads to the Barri Gòtic.

At the Ramblas end of the square, the inverted-staircase **monument** represents the shape of Catalunya and honors one of its former

Plaça de Catalunya—heart of the region

Proud monument to a Catalunyan president

Ramblas Ramble

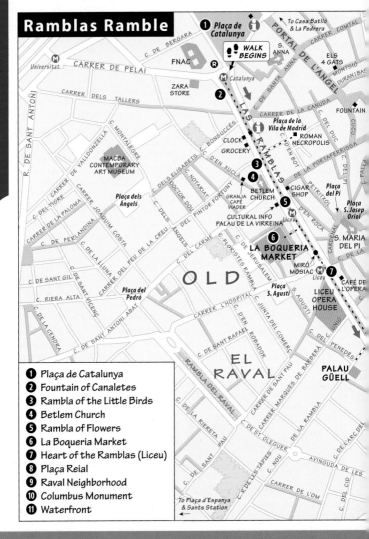

1. Plaça de Catalunya
2. Fountain of Canaletes
3. Rambla of the Little Birds
4. Betlem Church
5. Rambla of Flowers
6. La Boqueria Market
7. Heart of the Ramblas (Liceu)
8. Plaça Reial
9. Raval Neighborhood
10. Columbus Monument
11. Waterfront

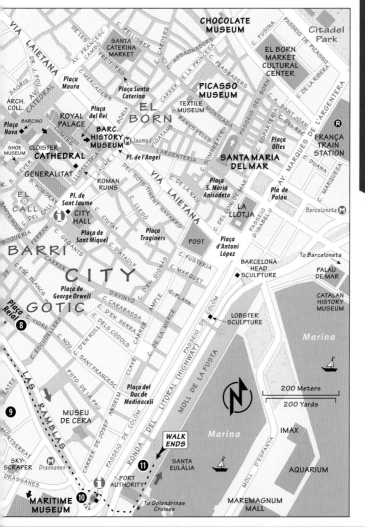

CHOCOLATE MUSEUM

Citadel Park

EL BORN MARKET CULTURAL CENTER

VIA LAIETANA

C. DE LES
AV. FRANCESC CAMBO

SANTA CATERINA MARKET

FREIXURES

C. PELLISSER

C. ASSAONADORS

C. CADERS

C. FLASSADERS

C. DE LA PRINCESA

C. FUSINA

PASSEIG DE PICASSO

C. DE LA RIBERA

SAGRIS
AV. CATEDRAL
DE J. POU

Plaça Maura

C. MERCADERS

Plaça Santa Caterina

PICASSO MUSEUM

MONTCADA

C. DE LA RIBERA

ARCH. COLL.

BARCINO

Plaça del Rei

EL BORN

TEXTILE MUSEUM

PASSEIG DEL BORN

C. SANT JOAN

PASSEIG DE L'ARGENTERA

ROYAL PALACE

BORIA

BANYS VELLS

ESPARTERIA

C. DE LES DELEC DE

FRANÇA TRAIN STATION

R

Plaça Nova

BARC. HISTORY MUSEUM

COMTES

Jaume I M

VIGATANS

L'ARGENTERIA

Plaça Olles

C. DUANA

SHOE MUSEUM

CLOISTER MUSEUM

CATHEDRAL

S. SEVER

LLIBRETERIA

JAUME I

Pl. de l'Angel

SANTA MARIA DEL MAR

C. MARQUESA

Barceloneta M

GENERALITAT

S. HONORAT

ROMAN RUINS

DEL SOTS-TINENT NAVARRO

Plaça S. Maria Anisadeta

C. DEL DON DE MAR

PASSEIG D'ISABEL II

EL CALL

C. DEL CALL

Pl. de Sant Jaume

VIA LAIETANA

LA LLOTJA

Pla de Palau

i

CITY HALL

C. CIUTAT

C. LLEDO

Plaça d'Antoni López

To Barceloneta

BARRI

POQUERIA

FERRAN

C. GEGANTS

Plaça de Sant Miquel

Plaça Traginers

POST

BARCELONA HEAD SCULPTURE

PALAU DE MAR

CITY

C. DATAULF

C. FUSTERIA

CATALAN HISTORY MUSEUM

GÒTIC

C. ESC. BLANCS

CARRER

D'EN GIGNAS

C. MARQUET

Plaça de George Orwell

D'AVINYO

C. PLATA

LOBSTER SCULPTURE

Marina

Plaça Reial

C. VIDRELLERS

C. CARABASSA

C. D'EN SERRA

PASSEIG DE COLOM

8

C. NOU D'EN RULL

C. DELS CODOLS

CLAVE CARRER

C. DE LA MERCE

RONDA DEL LITORAL (HIGHWAY)

MOLL DE LA FUSTA

200 Meters
200 Yards

9

PSTG. DE LA PAU

Plaça del Duc de Medinaceli

N

LAS RAMBLAS

MUSEU DE CERA

CARRER DE JOSEP ANSELM

PASSEIG DE COLOM

Marina

IMAX

MONTSERRAT

SKY-SCRAPER

M Drassanes

WALK ENDS

AQUARIUM

DRASSANES

10

11

PORT AUTHORITY

SANTA EULÀLIA

MOLL D'ESPANYA

MARITIME MUSEUM

To Golondrinas Cruises

MAREMAGNUM MALL

presidents, Francesc Macià i Llussà, who declared independence for the breakaway region in 1931. (It didn't quite stick.) Sculptor Josep Maria Subirachs, whose work you'll see at the Sagrada Família (✪ see page 98), designed this memorial.

The venerable Café Zürich, just across the street from the monument, is a popular downtown rendezvous spot for locals. Homesick Americans might prefer the nearby Hard Rock Café. The giant El Corte Inglés department store towering above the square (on the northeast side) has just about anything you might need.

▶ *Cross the street and start rambling down the Ramblas. To get oriented, pause 20 yards down, at the ornate lamppost with a fountain as its base (on the right, near #129).*

❷ Fountain of Canaletes

The black-and-gold **fountain** has been a local favorite for more than a century. When Barcelona tore down its medieval wall and transformed the Ramblas from a drainage ditch into an elegant promenade, this fountain was one of its early attractions. Legend says that a drink from the fountain ensures that you'll come back to Barcelona one day. Watch the tourists— eager to guarantee a return trip—struggle with the awkwardly high water pressure. It's still a popular let's-meet-at-the-fountain rendezvous spot and a gathering place for celebrations and demonstrations. Fans of the Barcelona soccer team rally here before a big match—some touch their hand to their lips, then "kiss" the fountain with their hand for good luck. It's also a good spot to fill up your water bottle.

As you survey the Ramblas action, get your bearings for our upcoming stroll. You'll see the following features here and all along the way:

The wavy **tile work** of the pavers underfoot represents the stream that once flowed here. *Rambla* means "stream" in Arabic, and this used to be a drainage ditch along the medieval wall of the Barri Gòtic. Many Catalan towns, established where rivers approach the sea, have streets called "Ramblas." Today Barcelona's "stream" has become a river of humanity.

Look up to see the city's characteristic shallow **balconies.** They're functional as well as decorative, with windows opening from floor to ceiling to allow more light and air into the tight, dark spaces of these cramped old buildings. The **plane trees** lining the boulevard are known for their peeling bark and hardiness in urban settings. These deciduous trees are

Fountain of Canaletes—popular rendezvous spot and a good luck charm for FC Barcelona fans

ideal for the climate, letting in maximum sun in the winter and providing maximum shade in the summer. Nowadays, fewer residents live around here—they've been supplanted by businesses and tourism. This shapes what's sold along the Ramblas: There are fewer flower shops and more market stalls catering to tourists.

Nearby, notice the **chairs** fixed to the sidewalk at jaunty angles. It used to be that you'd pay to rent a chair here to look at the constant parade of passersby. Seats are now free, and it's still the best people-watching in town. Enjoy these chairs while you can—you'll find virtually no public benches or other seating farther down the Ramblas, only cafés that serve beer and sangria in just one (expensive) size: *gigante*.

Across from the fountain and a few steps down, notice the first of many **ONCE booths** along this walk (pronounced OHN-thay, the Spanish "11"). These sell lottery tickets that support Spain's organization of the blind, a powerful advocate for the needs of people with disabilities.

▶ *Continue strolling.*

All along the Ramblas are **newsstands** (open 24 hours). Among their souvenirs, you'll see soccer paraphernalia, especially the scarlet-and-blue of FC Barcelona (known as "Barça"). The team is owned by its more than 170,000 "members"—fans who buy season tickets, which come with a share of ownership (the team's healthy payroll guarantees that they're always in contention). Their motto, "More than a club" *(Mes que un club),* suggests that Barça represents the entire Catalan cultural identity. This comes to a head during a match nicknamed "El Clásico," in which they face their bitter rivals, Real Madrid (whom many Barça fans view as stand-ins for Castilian cultural chauvinism).

Walk 100 yards downhill to #115, where the **Royal Academy of Science**'s clock marks official Barcelona time—synchronize. Notice the **TI** kiosk right on the Ramblas—a handy stop for any questions. The **Carrefour** supermarket just behind it has cheap groceries (at #113).

▶ *You're now standing at the...*

❸ Rambla of the Little Birds

Traditionally, kids brought their parents here to buy pets, especially on Sundays. Today, only one of the traditional pet kiosks survives—and there's not a bird in sight; you'll find mostly bird-related pet supplies and recorded chirping.

At #122 (the big, modern Citadines Hotel on the left, just behind the

"Barca" team colors stoke regional pride.

Betlem Church, a rare Baroque structure

pet kiosk), take a 100-yard detour through a passageway marked *Passage de la Ramblas* to find a **Roman necropolis.** Look down and imagine a 2,000-year-old tomb-lined road. In Roman cities, tombs (outside the walls) typically lined the roads leading into town. Emperor Augustus spent a lot of time in modern-day Spain conquering new land, so the Romans were sure to incorporate Hispania into the empire's infrastructure. This road, Via Augusta, led into the Roman port of Barcino (today's highway to France still follows the route laid out by this Roman thoroughfare). Looking down at these ruins, you can see how Roman Barcino was about 10 feet lower than today's street level.

▶ *Return to the Ramblas and continue 100 yards or so to the next street, Carrer de la Portaferrissa (across from the big church), turn left a few steps and look right to see the **decorative tile** over a fountain still in use by locals. The scene shows the original city wall with the gate that once stood here and the action on what is today's Ramblas. Nearby, note the Palau de la Virreina ticket office (La Rambla 99), a good one-stop-shopping place for concerts and events. Now cross the boulevard to the front of the big church.*

❹ Betlem Church

This 17th-century Baroque church is dedicated to Bethlehem, and for centuries locals have flocked here at Christmastime to see Nativity scenes. Check out the sloping roofline, ball-topped pinnacles, corkscrew columns, and scrolls above the entrance.

For a sweet treat, head around to the narrow lane on the far side of the church (running parallel to the Ramblas) to the recommended **Café Granja Viader,** which has specialized in baked and dairy delights since

1870. Step inside to see Viader family photos and early posters advertising Cacaolat—the local chocolate milk Barcelonans love.

▶ *Continue down the boulevard, through the stretch called the…*

❺ Rambla of Flowers

This colorful block is lined with flower stands. Gardeners will covet the seeds sold here for varieties of veggies seldom seen in the US—including the iconic green Padrón pepper of tapas fame (if you buy seeds, you must declare them to US customs when returning home). On the left, at #100, **Gimeno** sells cigars. Step inside and appreciate the dying art of cigar boxes. Go ahead, do something forbidden in America but perfectly legal here—buy a Cuban (little singles for €1). Tobacco shops sell stamps and phone cards, plus bongs and marijuana gear—the Spanish approach to pot is very casual. While people can't legally sell marijuana, they're allowed to grow it for personal use and consume it.

▶ *Continue to the Metro stop marked by the red M. At #91 (on the right) is the arcaded entrance to Barcelona's great covered market, La Boqueria. If this main entry is choked with visitors (as it often is), you can skirt around to a side entrance, one block in either direction (look for the round arches that mark passages into the market colonnade).*

❻ La Boqueria Market

This lively market hall is an explosion of chicken legs, bags of live snails, stiff fish, delicious oranges, odd odors, and sleeping dogs. The best day for a visit is Saturday, when the market is thriving. It's closed on Sundays,

Enjoy performers, but beware of pickpockets.

One segment of the "Ramblas" has flowers.

and locals avoid it on Mondays, when it's open but (they believe) vendors are selling items that aren't necessarily fresh.

Since as far back as 1200, Barcelonans have bought their animal parts here. The market was originally located by the walled city's entrance, as many medieval markets were (since it was more expensive to trade within the walls). It later expanded into the colonnaded courtyard of a now-gone monastery before being topped with a colorful arcade in 1850.

While tourists are drawn like moths to a flame to the area around the main entry (below the colorful stained-glass sign), you should explore deeper. The stalls up front pay the highest rent—and therefore have to inflate their prices. For example, the juice bars along the touristy main drag charge more than those a couple of aisles to the right.

Stop by the recommended **Pinotxo Bar**—it's just inside the market, under the sign—and snap a photo of animated Juan giving a thumbs-up for your camera. The stools nearby are a fine perch for enjoying both your coffee and the people-watching.

The market and lanes nearby are busy with tempting little eateries (✪ see page 149). Drop by a café for an *espresso con leche* or breakfast *tortilla española* (potato omelet). The small square on the north side of the

La Boqueria entrance—the arcade hosts vendors of seafood, produce, and hocks of *jamón*.

market hosts a farmers' market in the mornings. Wander around—as local architect Antoni Gaudí used to—and gain inspiration. Go on a scavenger hunt.

Produce stands show off seasonal fruits and vegetables. ("Market cuisine" is big at Barcelona restaurants—chefs come to markets like this each morning to rustle up ingredients.) The tubs of little green peppers that look like jalapeños are lightly fried for the dish called *pimientos de Padrón*. In the fall, you'll see lots of mushrooms; in the winter, artichokes.

Full legs of *jamón* (ham)—some costing upwards of €200—tempt the Spaniards who so love this local delicacy. You'll see many types of the Catalan specialty sausage *botifarra*. Some can be eaten as is, others must be cooked. You'll also find *chorizo* (red, sometimes spicy sausage) and gamier meats such as rabbit and suckling pig. *Huevos del toro* are bull testicles—surprisingly inexpensive...and oh so good.

The **fishmonger** stalls could double as a marine biology lab. Notice that fish is sold whole, not filleted—local shoppers like to look their dinner in the eye to be sure it's fresh. Count the many different types of shrimp (*gamba, scampi, langostino,* clawed *cigala*). One of the weirdest Spanish edibles is the tubular razor clam *(navaja de almeja),* with something oozing out of each end. **Salt cod** *(bacalao)* is preserved and dried. Before it can be eaten, it must be rehydrated. Historically, this provided desperately needed protein on long sea voyages.

Olives are a keystone of the Spanish diet. Take a look at the 25 kinds offered at the **Graus Olives i Conserves** shop (straight in, near the back).

▶ *Head back out to the street and continue down the Ramblas.*

You're skirting the western boundary of the old Barri Gòtic neighborhood. As you walk, glance to the left through a modern cutaway arch for

Of the market's many vendors, here's Juan.

The market is a photographic wonderland.

Fresh seafood, base of Barcelonan cuisine   Mosaic by hometown boy Joan Miró

a glimpse of the medieval church tower of **Santa Maria del Pi,** a popular venue for guitar concerts (✪ see page 174). This also marks Plaça del Pi and a great shopping street, Carrer Petritxol, which runs parallel to the Ramblas (see "Shopping Neighborhoods" in the Practicalities chapter).

Now look across to the other side of the Ramblas. At the corner, find the highly regarded **Escribà** bakery, with its fine Modernista facade and interior (look for the *Antigua Casa Figueras* sign arching over the doorway). Notice the beautiful mosaics of twining plants, the stained glass, and the fine woodwork. On the sidewalk in front of the door, a plaque dates the building to 1902 (plaques like this identify historic shops all over town).

▸ *After another block, you reach the Liceu Metro station, marking the...*

❼ Heart of the Ramblas (Liceu)

At the Liceu Metro station's elevators, the Ramblas widens a bit into a small, lively square (Plaça de la Boqueria). Liceu marks the midpoint of the Ramblas, halfway between Plaça de Catalunya and the waterfront.

Underfoot in the center of the Ramblas, find the much-trod-upon red-white-yellow-and-blue **mosaic** by homegrown abstract artist Joan Miró. The mosaic's black arrow represents an anchor, a reminder of the city's attachment to the sea. Miró's simple, colorful designs are found all over the city, from murals to mobiles to the La Caixa bank logo. The best place in Barcelona to see his work is in the Fundació Joan Miró at Montjuïc (✪ see page 129).

The surrounding buildings have playful ornamentation typical of the city. The **Chinese dragon** holding a lantern (at #82) decorates a former umbrella shop (notice the fun umbrella mosaics high up). The dragon is an

Fanciful decorations on buildings, like this one near Liceu Metro, are part of Barcelona's charm.

important symbol of Catalan pride for its connection to the city's dragon-slaying patron saint, St. George (Jordi).

Hungry? Swing around the back of the umbrella shop to the recommended **Taverna Basca Irati** tapas bar (a block up Carrer del Cardenal Casanyes). This is one of many user-friendly, Basque-style tapas bars in town; instead of ordering, you can just grab or point to what looks good on the display platters, then pay per piece.

Back on the Ramblas, a few steps down (on the right) is the **Liceu Opera House** (Gran Teatre del Liceu), which hosts world-class opera, dance, and theater (box office around the right side, open Mon-Fri 13:30-20:00). Opposite the opera house is Café de l'Opera (#74), an elegant stop for an expensive beverage. This bustling café, with Modernista decor and a historic atmosphere, boasts that it's been open since 1929, even during the Spanish Civil War.

▶ *We've seen the best stretch of the Ramblas. To cut this walk short, you could catch the Metro back to Plaça de Catalunya. Otherwise, let's continue to the port. The wide, straight street that crosses the Ramblas in another 30 yards (Carrer de Ferran) leads left to Plaça de Sant Jaume, the government center.*

Head down the Ramblas another 50 yards (to #46), and turn left down an arcaded lane (Carrer de Colom) to the square called...

❽ Plaça Reial

Dotted with palm trees, surrounded by an arcade, and ringed by yellow buildings with white Neoclassical trim, this elegant square has a colonial ambience. It comes with old-fashioned taverns, modern bars with patio seating, and a Sunday coin-and-stamp market. Completing the picture are Gaudí's first public works (the two colorful helmeted lampposts). While this used to be a seedy and dangerous part of town, recent gentrification efforts have given it new life, making it inviting and accessible. (The small streets stretching toward the water from the square remain a bit sketchier.) It's a lively hangout by day or by night (for nightlife options, ✪ see page 174). Big spaces like this (as well as the site of La Boqueria Market) often originated as monasteries. When these were dissolved in the 19th century, their fine colonnaded squares were incorporated into useful public spaces. To relax over a drink and enjoy the scene, the **Ocaña cocktail bar** is a good bet.

▶ *Head back out to the Ramblas.*

Across the boulevard, a half-block detour down Carrer Nou de la Rambla brings you to **Palau Güell,** designed by Antoni Gaudí (on the left, at #3). Recently renovated, Palau Güell offers an informative look at a

Plaça Reial—a lively hangout

Palau Güell—parabolic arches by Gaudí

Gaudí interior (✪ see listing on page 110). Pablo Picasso had a studio at #10 (though there's nothing to see there today).

▶ *Proceed along the Ramblas.*

❾ Raval Neighborhood

The neighborhood on the right-hand side of this stretch of the Ramblas is El Raval. In the last century, this was a rough neighborhood, home to sailors, prostitutes, and poor immigrants. Today, it's becoming gentrified, but it's still pretty dodgy.

The **street performers** you'll likely see—such as the goofy human statues—must audition and register with the city government; to avoid overcrowding, only 15 can work along the Ramblas at any one time. Dropping a coin in their can often kicks the statues into entertaining gear. Warning: Wherever people stop to gawk, pickpockets are at work.

You're also likely to see some old-fashioned shell games in this part of town. Stand back and observe these nervous no-necks at work. They swish around their little boxes, making sure to show you the pea. Their shills play and win. Then, in hopes of making easy money, fools lose big time.

Near the bottom of the Ramblas, take note of the **Drassanes Metro stop,** which can take you back to Plaça de Catalunya when this walk is over. The skyscraper to the right of the Ramblas is the Edificio Colón. When it was built in 1970, the 28-story structure was Barcelona's first high-rise. Near the skyscraper is the Maritime Museum, housed in what were the city's giant medieval shipyards (✪ see page 111).

▶ *Up ahead is the...*

❿ Columbus Monument

The 200-foot column honors Christopher Columbus, who came to Barcelona in 1493 after journeying to America. This Catalan answer to Nelson's Column on London's Trafalgar Square (right down to the lions perfect for posing with at the base) was erected for the 1888 Universal Exposition, an international fair that helped vault a surging Barcelona onto the world stage.

The base of the monument, ringed with four winged victories (taking flight to the four corners of the earth), is loaded with symbolism: statues and reliefs of mapmakers, navigators, early explorers preaching to subservient Native Americans, and (enthroned just below the winged

The Columbus Monument, located where the Ramblas meets the sea, honors a man with Barcelona ties.

victories) the four regions of Spain. The reliefs near the bottom illustrate scenes from Columbus' fateful voyage. It's ironic that Barcelona so celebrates this explorer; the discoveries of Columbus started 300 years of decline for the city, as Europe began to face West (the Atlantic and the New World) rather than East (the Mediterranean and the Orient). Within a few decades of Columbus, Barcelona had become a depressed backwater, and didn't rebound until events like the 1888 Expo cemented its status as a comeback city.

A tiny elevator ascends to the top of the monument, lifting visitors to a glassed-in observation area for fine panoramas over the city (entrance/ticket desk in TI inside the base of the monument).

▶ *Scoot across the busy traffic circle to survey the...*

⑪ Waterfront

Stand on the boardwalk (between the modern bridge and the kiosks selling harbor cruises), and survey Barcelona's bustling maritime zone. Although the city is one of Europe's top 10 ports, with many busy industrial harbors and several cruise terminals, this low-impact stretch of seafront is clean, fresh, and people-friendly.

A wave-like pedestrian bridge over the harbor leads to the Maremagnum shopping mall.

As you face the water, the frilly yellow building to your left is the fanciful Modernista-style port-authority building. The wooden pedestrian **bridge** jutting straight out into the harbor is a modern extension of the Ramblas. Called La Rambla de Mar ("Rambla of the Sea"), the bridge swings out to allow boat traffic into the marina; when closed, the footpath leads to an entertainment and shopping complex. Just to your right are the *golondrinas* **harbor cruise** boats, which can be fun (though the views from the harbor aren't great; for details, ✪ see page 112).

▶ *Turn left and walk 100 yards along the promenade between the port authority and the harbor.*

This delightful promenade is part of Barcelona's **Old Port** (Port Vell). The port's pleasant sailboat marina is completely enclosed by a modern complex with the Maremagnum shopping mall, an IMAX cinema, a huge aquarium, restaurants, and piles of people. Along the promenade is a permanently moored historic schooner, the *Santa Eulália* (part of the Maritime Museum—✪ see page 111).

Imagine: Nearly three decades ago, this was a gloomy, depressed warehouse zone. It was refurbished for the 1992 Olympics. City leaders routed a busy highway underground to create this fine walkway sprinkled with palm trees and eye-pleasing public art.

From here, you can pick out some of Barcelona's more distant charms. The triangular spit of land across the harbor is the neighborhood of **Barceloneta**—a somewhat gritty but charming area, popular for its easy access to an inviting stretch of broad, sandy beaches. Looking back toward the Columbus Monument, in the distance you'll see the majestic, 570-foot bluff of **Montjuïc,** dotted with a number of sights and museums (✪ see page 125).

▶ *Your ramble is over. To reach other points in town, your best bet is to backtrack to the Drassanes Metro stop, at the bottom of the Ramblas. Alternatively, you can catch buses #14 or #59 from along the top of the promenade back to Plaça de Catalunya.*

Barri Gòtic Walk

From Plaça de Catalunya to Plaça del Rei

Barcelona's Barri Gòtic (Gothic Quarter) is a bustling world of shops, bars, and nightlife packed into narrow, winding lanes and undiscovered court-yards. This is Barcelona's birthplace—where the ancient Romans built a city, where medieval Christians constructed their cathedral, where Jews gathered together, and where Barcelonans lived within a ring of protective walls until the 1850s, when the city expanded.

Today, the area—"El Gòtic"—is historic and atmospheric. It's a grab bag of grand squares, classy antique shops, wrought-iron balconies, and street musicians strumming Catalan folk songs. In the center of it all is the cathedral, surrounded by other legacy sights from the city's medieval era. Use this walk to get the lay of the land, then explore the shopping streets nearby (✪ see page 173) or head to El Born (✪ see page 114).

ORIENTATION

Length of This Walk: Figure 1.5 hours, not including entering sights such as the cathedral.

When to Go: If you want to visit the cathedral when admission is free, take this walk in the morning or late afternoon. Some sights mentioned on this walk are closed Monday.

Getting There: Start at the southeast corner of the Plaça de Catalunya (Metro: Plaça de Catalunya).

Church of Santa Anna: €2, generally open Mon-Fri 11:00-19:00, closed Sat-Sun, Plazoleta de Santa Anna.

Cathedral of Barcelona: Generally free except in afternoon, open Mon-Fri 8:00-19:30, Sat-Sun 8:00-20:00, €7 to enter Mon-Sat 13:00-17:00 and Sun 14:00-17:00, Plaça de la Seu. For details, ✪ see the Cathedral of Barcelona Tour chapter.

Old Main Synagogue: €2.50, Mon-Fri 10:30-18:00, Sat-Sun 10:30-15:00, shorter hours off-season, Carrer Marlet 5, tel. 931-170-790, www.calldebarcelona.org.

Roman Temple of Augustus: Free, daily 10:00-19:00, except Mon until 14:00, Carrer del Paradís 10.

Barcelona History Museum: €7, Tue-Sat 10:00-19:00, Sun 10:00-20:00, closed Mon, off Plaça del Rei.

Eating: For suggestions, ✪ see page 150.

THE WALK BEGINS

▶ *Start on Barcelona's grand main square,* **Plaça de Catalunya** *(✪ described on page 17 of the Ramblas Ramble chapter). From the northeast corner (between the giant El Corte Inglés department store and the Banco de España), head down the broad pedestrian boulevard called...*

❶ Avinguda del Portal de l'Angel

For much of Barcelona's history, this was a major city gate. A medieval wall enclosed the city, and there was an entrance here—the "Gate of the Angel"—that gives the street its name. An angel statue atop the gate purportedly kept the city safe from plagues and bid voyagers safe journey as they left the security of the city.

The street (like many other areas of the city) got periodic facelifts whenever Barcelona held events that welcomed the world: the 1888 Universal Exposition (that also gave us the Columbus Monument), the 1929 World's Fair (that created Plaça d'Espanya), and the 1992 Olympic Games (that rejuvenated Montjuïc and the waterfront).

Today, this formerly traffic-choked street welcomes shoppers cruising some of the most expensive retail spaces in town. It's pretty globalized and sanitized, with lots of high-end Spanish and international chains (for a brief rundown, ✪ see page 174), but a handful of businesses with local roots survive. At the first corner (at #21), a green sign marks **Planelles Donat**—long appreciated for its ice cream, sweet *turró* (or *turrón,* almond-and-honey candy), refreshing *orxata* (or *horchata,* almond-flavored drink), and *granissat* (or *granizado,* ice slush).

▶ *A block farther down, pause at Carrer de Santa Anna to admire the Art Nouveau awning at another El Corte Inglés department store. From here, take a half-block detour to the right on Carrer de Santa Anna. At #32 go through a large entryway into a pleasant, flower-fragrant courtyard with the...*

❷ Church of Santa Anna

This 12th-century gem was an *extra* muro ("outside the walls") church; look for its marker cross still standing outside. Because it was part of a convent, the church has a fine cloister—an arcaded walkway around a leafy courtyard (viewable to the left of the church). Climb the modern stairs for views of the bell tower. If the church is open, you'll see a bare Romanesque

Barri Gòtic Walk

WALK BEGINS

To Casa Batlló & La Pedrera

Plaça de Catalunya

PLANELLES DONAT

CARRER D'ESTRUC

C. DE LES MOLES

CARRER COMTAL

SANTA ANNA

CONDOM SHOP

ELS QUATRE GATS

AVINGUDA DEL PORTAL DE L'ANGEL

CARRER DE MONTSIÓ

FNAC

Catalunya

Catalunya

CARRER DE SANTA ANNA

BARRI

LOANER BIKES

CARRER DE LA CANUDA

CARRER CUCURULLA

Plaça de la Vila de Madrid

ROMAN NECRÒPOLIS

GÒTIC

CARRER DEL DUC

CARRER D'EN BOT

CARRER BONSUCCÈS

CLOCK

CARRER DE LA PORTAFERRISSA

CARRER DEL PI

LAS RAMBLAS

CARRER D'EN XUCLÀ

BETLEM CHURCH

CULTURAL INFO PALAU DE LA VIRREINA

VICENS SWEETS

GRANJA LA PALLARESA (CHURROS CON CHOCOLATE)

CARRER D'EN ROCA

PETRITXOL

JOSEP ROCA CUTLERY

100 Meters

100 Yards

To La Boqueria Market, Columbus Monument & Harbor

Liceu

Plaça del Pi

Plaça S. Josep Oriol

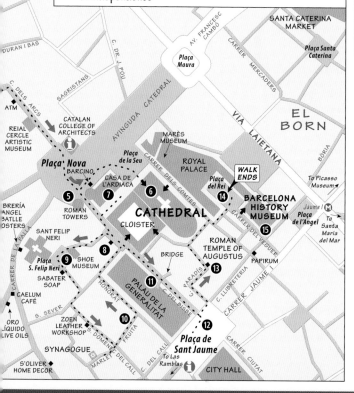

1. Avinguda del Portal de l'Angel
2. Church of Santa Anna
3. Els Quatre Gats Rest.
4. Fountain
5. Plaça Nova
6. Cathedral of Barcelona
7. Casa de l'Ardiaca
8. Monument to the Martyrs of Independence
9. Plaça Sant Felip Neri
10. Jewish Quarter
11. Carrer del Bisbe Bridge
12. Plaça de Sant Jaume
13. Roman Temple of Augustus
14. Plaça del Rei
15. Barcelona History Museum

interior and Greek-cross floor plan, topped with an octagonal wooden roof. The recumbent-knight tomb is that of Miguel de Boera, renowned admiral of Charles V. The door at the far end of the nave leads to the cloister.

As you head back to the main drag, you'll pass—a few doors down—a **condom shop** on your left. It advertises (to men with ample self-esteem): *Para los pequeños placeres de la vida* ("For the little pleasures in life").

▶ *Backtrack to Avingunda del Portal de l'Angel. At Carrer de Montsió (on the left), opposite the Zara store, side-trip half a block to...*

❸ Els Quatre Gats

This restaurant ("The Four Cats"), established in 1897, is a historic monument, tourist attraction, nightspot, and recommended eatery. It's famous for being the circa-1900 bohemian-artist hangout where Picasso nursed drinks with friends and had his first one-man show (in 1900). The building itself, by prominent Catalan architect Josep Puig i Cadafalch, represents Neo-Gothic Modernisme. Stepping inside, you feel the turn-of-the-century vibe. Rich Barcelona elites and would-be avant-garde artists looked to Paris, not Madrid, for cultural inspiration. Consequently, this place was clearly inspired by the Paris scene (especially Le Chat Noir cabaret/café, the hangout of Montmartre intellectuals). Like Le Chat Noir, Els Quatre Gats even published its own artsy magazine for a while. The story of the name? When the proprietor told his friends that he'd stay open 24 hours a day, they said, "No one will come. It'll just be you and four cats" (Catalan slang for "just a few people"). While you can have a snack, meal, or drink here, you're welcome to just admire the menu cover art—originally painted by Picasso—and take a quick look around (ask *"Solo mirar, por favor?"*).

▶ *Return to and continue down Avingunda del Portal de l'Angel. In a square on the left, notice the rack of city loaner bikes, part of the popular and successful "Bicing" program designed to reduce car traffic (available only to Barcelona residents). You'll soon reach a fork in the road and a building with a...*

❹ Fountain

The blue-and-yellow tilework, a circa-1918 addition to this even older fountain, depicts ladies carrying jugs of water. In the 17th century, this was the last watering stop for horses before leaving town. As recently as 1940, one in nine Barcelonans got their water from fountains like this. It's still used today.

▶ *Shoppers will feel the pull of wonderful little shops down the street to the right. But be strong and take the left fork, down Carrer dels Arcs.*

Pause after a few steps at the yellow La Caixa ATM (on the right, under the terrace). Touch the screen to see various languages pop up—in addition to English, French, and German, you'll see the **four languages of Spain** and their flags: Català (Catalan; thin red-and-gold stripes), Galego (Galicia, in northwest Spain; white with a diagonal blue slash), Castellano (Español or Spanish; broad red, yellow, and red bands), and Euskara (Basque; red, green, and white). As a would-be breakaway nation fiercely proud of its own customs and language, Catalunya is in solidarity with other small ethnic groups. Catalans are sure to include Basque here, for instance, just as they'd expect to see Catalan on ATMs in Basque Country.

Just past the ATM, you'll pass the Reial Cercle Artístic Museum, a private collection of Dalí's work—sculptures, prints, and lithographs.

▶ *Enter the large square called...*

❺ Plaça Nova

Two bold **Roman towers** flank the main street. These once guarded the entrance gate of the ancient Roman city of Barcino. The big stones that make up the base of the (reconstructed) towers are actually Roman. Near the base of the left tower, **modern bronze letters** spell out "BARCINO." The city's name may have come from Barca, one of Hannibal's generals, who is said to have passed through during Hannibal's roundabout invasion of Italy. At Barcino's peak, the **Roman wall** (see the section stretching to the left of the towers) was 25 feet high and a mile around, with 74 towers. It enclosed a population of 4,000.

Old tilework fountain along the Avinguda

Two ancient Roman towers on Plaça Nova

Frieze by Barcelona's own Pablo Picasso

Cathedral—medieval core, 19th-century facade

One of the towers has a bit of reconstructed **Roman aqueduct** (notice the stream bed on top). In ancient times, these bridges of stone carried fresh water from the distant hillsides into the walled city.

Opposite the towers is the modern **Catalan College of Architects** building (Collegi d'Arquitectes de Barcelona, TI inside), which is, ironically for a city with so much great architecture, quite ugly. The frieze was designed by Picasso (1962) in his distinctive simplified style, showing (on three sides) Catalan traditions: shipping, music, the *sardana* dance, bullfighting, and branch-waving kings and children celebrating a local festival. Picasso spent his formative years (1895-1904, ages 14-23) here in the old town. He drank with fellow bohemians at Els Quatre Gats and frequented brothels a few blocks from here on Carrer d'Avinyó ("Avignon")—which inspired his influential Cubist painting *Les Demoiselles d'Avignon*. Picasso's hunger to be on the cutting edge propelled him from the Barri Gòtic to Paris, where he eventually remade modern art.

▶ Head left through Plaça Nova and take in the mighty facade of the...

⑥ Cathedral of Barcelona

While this location has been a center of Christian worship since the fourth century, what you see today dates (mainly) from the 14th century, with a 19th-century Neo-Gothic facade. The facade is a virtual catalog of Gothic motifs: a pointed arch over the entrance, robed statues, tracery in windows, gargoyles, and bell towers with winged angels. This Gothic variation is called French Flamboyant (meaning "flame-like"), and the roofline sports the prickly spires meant to give the impression of a church flickering with spiritual fires. The area in front of the cathedral is where Barcelonans dance the *sardana* (✿ see page 112).

The cathedral's interior—with its vast size, peaceful cloister, and many ornate chapels—is worth a visit. For a walk through the cathedral's interior, ✪ see the Cathedral of Barcelona Tour chapter. (If you interrupt this tour and visit the cathedral now, you'll exit from the cloister a block down Carrer del Bisbe. From there you can circle back to the right to visit stop #7—or skip #7 and step directly into stop #8.)

▶ As you stand in the square facing the cathedral, look far to your left to see the multicolored, wavy canopy marking the roofline of the **Santa Caterina Market,** which is at the edge of the **El Born** neighborhood (✪ see page 114). To the right of the cathedral, at the far end of the square, is Carrer de la Palla, a good starting point for **shopping** in the Barri Gòtic (for recommendations, ✪ see page 173).

For now, return to the Roman towers. Pass between the towers to head up Carrer del Bisbe, and take an immediate left, up the ramp to the entrance of the...

❼ Casa de l'Ardiaca

It's free to enter this mansion, which was once the archdeacon's residence and now functions as the city archives. The elaborately carved doorway is Renaissance. To the right of the doorway is a carved mail slot by 19th-century Modernista architect Lluís Domènech i Montaner. Enter a small courtyard with a fountain. Notice how the century-old palm tree seems to be held captive by urban man. Next, step inside the lobby of the city archives, where there are often free temporary exhibits. At the left end of the lobby, go through the archway and look down into the stairwell—this is the back side of the ancient Roman wall. Back in the courtyard, climb

Casa de l'Ardiaca's Modernista mail slot

Monument to the Martyrs of Independence

to the balcony for views of the cathedral steeple and gargoyles. From this vantage point, note the small Romanesque chapel on the right (the only surviving 13th-century bit of the cathedral) and how it's dwarfed by the towering cathedral.

▶ *Return to Carrer del Bisbe and turn left. After a few steps, you reach a small square with a bronze statue ensemble.*

❽ Monument to the Martyrs of Independence

Five Barcelona patriots—including two priests—calmly receive their last rites before being garrotted (strangled) for resisting Napoleon's occupation of Spain in the early 19th century. They'd been outraged by French atrocities in Madrid (depicted in Goya's famous *Third of May* painting in Madrid's Prado Museum). According to the plaque marking their mortal remains, these martyrs to independence gave their lives in 1809 *"por Dios, por la Patria, y por el Rey"*—for God, country, and king.

The plaza offers interesting views of the cathedral's towers. Opposite the square is the "back door" entrance to the cathedral (through the cloister; relatively uncrowded and open sporadically).

On this square (and throughout the Barri Gòtic), you're likely to see immigrants selling knickknacks on the street, along with groups of hippies—nicknamed the "dog-and-flute people."

▶ *Exit the square down tiny Carrer de Montjuïc del Bisbe (to the right as you face the martyrs). This leads to the cute...*

❾ Plaça Sant Felip Neri

This shaded square serves as the playground of an elementary school and is often bursting with energetic kids speaking Catalan (just a generation ago, this would have been illegal and they would be speaking Spanish). The Church of Sant Felip Neri, which Gaudí attended, is still pocked with bomb damage from the Spanish Civil War. As a stronghold of democratic, anti-Franco forces, Barcelona saw a lot of fighting. The shrapnel that damaged this church was meant for the nearby Catalan government building (Palau de la Generalitat, which we'll see later on this walk).

The fascist friends of Franco (both German and Italian) helped bomb Barcelona from the air. A second bombing followed the first as survivors combed the rubble for lost loved ones. A plaque on the wall (left of church door) honors the 42 killed—mostly children—in that 1938 aerial bombardment.

The Church of Sant Felip Neri still shows bomb damage from Spain's bitter Civil War of the 1930s.

The buildings here were paid for by the guilds that powered the local economy (notice the carved reliefs high above). The corner where you entered the square is the former home of the shoemakers' guild; today it's the fun little **Shoe Museum** (✪ described on page 113). Also fronting the square is the **Sabater Hermanos** artisanal soap shop.

▶ *Exit the square down Carrer de Sant Felip Neri. At the T-intersection, turn right onto Carrer de Sant Sever, then immediately left on Carrer de Sant Domènec del Call (look for the blue El Call sign). You've entered the...*

➓ Jewish Quarter (El Call)

In Catalan, a Jewish quarter goes by the name El Call—literally "narrow passage," for the tight lanes where medieval Jews were forced to live, under the watchful eye of the nearby cathedral. (Or some believe El Call comes from the Hebrew *kahal,* which means congregation.) At the peak of Barcelona's El Call, some 4,000 Jews were crammed into just a few alleys in this neighborhood.

Walk down Carrer de Sant Domènec del Call, passing the **Zoen leather workshop and showroom,** where everything is made on the spot (on the right, at #15). Pass through the charming little square (a gap in the dense tangle of medieval buildings cleared by a civil war bomb), where you will find a rust-colored sign displaying a map of the Jewish Quarter. Take the next lane to the right (Carrer de Marlet). On the right is the low-profile entrance to what was likely Barcelona's **main synagogue** during the Middle Ages (Antigua Sinagoga Mayor). The structure dates from the third century, but it was destroyed during a brutal pogrom in 1391. The city's remaining Jews were expelled in 1492, and artifacts of their culture—including this synagogue—were forgotten for centuries. In the 1980s, a historian tracked down the synagogue using old tax-collection records. Another clue that this was the main synagogue: In accordance with Jewish traditions, it stubbornly faces east (toward Jerusalem), putting it at an angle at odds with surrounding structures. The sparse interior includes access to two small subterranean rooms with Roman walls topped by a medieval Catalan vault. Look through the glass floor to see dyeing vats used for a later shop on this site (run by former Jews who had been forcibly converted to Christianity).

▶ *From the synagogue, start back the way you came but continue straight ahead, onto Carrer de la Fruita. At the T-intersection, turn left, then right,*

Carrer del Bisbe has a Neo-Gothic look.

Catalunya's autonomous seat of government

to find your way back to the Martyrs statue. From here, turn right down Carrer del Bisbe, likely passing a street musician (the city gives permits for quality buskers to perform at set points like this one), to the...

⑪ Carrer del Bisbe Bridge

This structure—reminiscent of Venice's Bridge of Sighs—connects the Catalan government building (on the right) with what was the Catalan president's ceremonial residence (on the left). Though the bridge looks medieval, it was constructed in the 1920s by Catalan architect Joan Rubió (a follower of Gaudí), who also did the carved ornamentation on the buildings.

Check out the jutting angels on the bridge, the basket-carrying maidens on the president's house, and the gargoyle-like faces on the government building. Find monsters, skulls, goddesses, old men with beards, climbing vines, and coats of arms. The delicate facade a few steps farther down on the right marks the 15th-century entry to the government palace.

▶ *Continue along Carrer del Bisbe to...*

⑫ Plaça de Sant Jaume

This stately central square of the Barri Gòtic takes its name from the Church of St. James (in Catalan: Jaume, "JOW-mah") that once stood here. After the church was torn down in 1823, the square was fixed up and rechristened "Plaça de la Constitució" in honor of the then decade-old Spanish constitution. But the plucky Catalans never embraced the name, and after Franco, they went back to the original title—even though the namesake church is long gone.

Set at the intersection of ancient Barcino's main thoroughfares, this square was once a Roman forum. In that sense, it's been the seat of city government for 2,000 years. Today it's home to the two top governmental buildings in Catalunya: Palau de la Generalitat, and across from it, the Barcelona City Hall.

For more than six centuries, the **Palau de la Generalitat** (to your immediate right as you enter the square) has housed the offices of the autonomous government of Catalunya. It always flies the Catalan flag next to the obligatory Spanish one. Above the building's doorway is Catalunya's patron saint—St. George (Jordi), slaying the dragon. The dragon (which you'll see all over town) is an important Catalan symbol. From these balconies, the nation's leaders (and soccer heroes) greet the people on momentous days. The square is often the site of demonstrations, from a single aggrieved citizen with a megaphone (the phone company billed me twice!) to riotous thousands (demanding independence from Spain, for instance).

Facing the Generalitat across the square is the **Barcelona City Hall** (Casa de la Ciutat). It sports a statue (in the niche to the left of the door) of a different James—"Jaume el Conqueridor." The 13th-century King Jaume I is credited with freeing Barcelona from French control, granting self-government, and setting it on a course to become a major city. He was the driving force behind construction of the Royal Palace (which we'll see shortly).

Locals treasure the independence these two government buildings represent. In the 20th century, Barcelona opposed the dictator Francisco Franco (who ruled from 1939 to 1975), and Franco retaliated. He abolished the regional government and (effectively) outlawed the Catalan language and customs. Two years after Franco's death, joyous citizens packed this square to celebrate the return of self-rule.

Look left and right down the main streets branching off the square; they're lined with ironwork streetlamps and balconies draped with plants. Carrer de Ferran, which leads to the Ramblas, is classic Barcelona.

In ancient Roman days, when Plaça de Sant Jaume was the town's central square, two main streets converged here—the Decumanus (Carrer del Bisbe—bishop's street) and the Cardus (Carrer de la Llibreteria/Carrer del Call). The forum's biggest building was a massive temple of Augustus, which we'll see next.

▸ *Facing the Generalitat, exit the square going up the second street to the right of the building, on tiny Carrer del Paradís. Follow this street as it turns right. When it swings left, pause at #10, the entrance to the...*

Impressive remains of a 2,000-year-old Roman temple that once stood facing Plaça Jaume

⑬ Roman Temple of Augustus

You're standing at the summit of Mont Tàber, the Barri Gòtic's highest spot. A plaque on the wall reads: "Mont Tàber, 16.9 meters" (elevation 55 feet). A millstone inlaid in the pavement at the doorstep of #10 also marks the spot. It was here that the ancient Romans founded the town of Barcino around 15 B.C. They built a *castrum* (fort) on the hilltop, protecting the harbor.

Go inside for a peek at the last vestiges of an imposing Roman temple (Temple Roma d'August, pictured on previous page). All that's left now are four columns and some fragments of the transept and its plinth (good English info on-site). The huge columns, dating from the late first century B.C., are as old as Barcelona itself. They were part of the ancient town's biggest structure, a temple dedicated to the Emperor Augustus, who was worshipped as a god. These Corinthian columns (with deep fluting and topped with leafy capitals) were the back corner of a 120-foot-long temple that extended from here to Barcino's forum.

▶ *Continue down Carrer del Paradís one block. When you bump into the back end of the cathedral, take a right, and go downhill a block (down Carrer de la Pietat/Baixada de Santa Clara) until you emerge into a square called...*

⑭ Plaça del Rei

The buildings enclosing this square exemplify Barcelona's medieval past. The central section (topped by a five-story addition) was the core of the **Royal Palace** (Palau Reial Major). A vast hall on its ground floor once served as the throne room and reception room. From the 13th to the 15th century, the Royal Palace housed Barcelona's counts as well as the

Palace (center), Chapel (r), Viceroy (l)

Barcelona History Museum

resident kings of Aragon. In 1493, a triumphant Christopher Columbus, accompanied by six New World natives (whom he called *"indios"*) and several pure-gold statues, entered the Royal Palace. King Ferdinand and Queen Isabella rose to welcome him home and honored him with the title "Admiral of the Oceans."

To the right is the palace's church, the 14th-century **Chapel of Saint Agatha,** which sits atop the foundations of a Roman wall (entrance included in Barcelona History Museum admission; ✪ see page 114).

To the left is the **Viceroy's Palace** (Palau del Lloctinent, for the ruler's right-hand man). This 16th-century building currently serves as the archives of the Crown of Aragon. After Catalunya became part of Spain in the 15th century, the Royal Palace became a small regional residence, and the Viceroy's Palace became the headquarters of the local Inquisition. Step inside to see the delightful Renaissance courtyard, a staircase with coffered wood ceilings, and a temporary exhibit space. Among the archive's treasures (though it's rarely on display) is the 1492 Santa Fe Capitulations, a contract between Columbus and the monarchs about his upcoming sea voyage. (See the poster of the yellowed document on the wall outside, with an English explanation.)

Ironically, Columbus' discovery of new trade routes (abandoning the Mediterranean for the Atlantic) made Barcelona's port less important, and soon the royals moved elsewhere.

▶ *From the square, go downhill onto Carrer del Veguer, where you'll find the entrance to the...*

⓯ Barcelona History Museum

This museum contains primarily objects from archaeological digs around Barcelona. But the real highlight is underground, where you can examine excavated Roman ruins. (For details on the museum, ✪ see page 114).

▶ *Your walk is over. It's easy to get your bearings by backtracking to either Plaça de Sant Jaume or the cathedral. The Jaume I Metro stop is two blocks away (leave the square on Carrer del Veguer and turn left). From here, you're within striking distance of El Born (✪ see page 114), the Picasso Museum (✪ see page 117), or Barri Gòtic shopping (✪ see page 173). Or simply wander and enjoy Barcelona at its Gothic best.*

Cathedral of Barcelona Tour

Although Barcelona's cathedral doesn't rank among Europe's finest (and frankly, barely cracks the Top 20), it is important, easy to visit, and—much of the time—free to see. This quick tour introduces you to the cathedral's highlights: its vast nave, rich chapels, tomb of St. Eulàlia, and the oasis-like setting of the cloister. Other sights inside (which you'll pay separately for) are the elaborately carved choir, the elevator up to the view terrace, and the altarpiece museum.

ORIENTATION

Cost: Free in the morning (Mon-Sat before 12:45, Sun before 13:45) and late afternoon (after 17:15), but you have to pay for the cathedral's three minor sights—choir-€3, elevator to terrace-€3, and museum-€2. Although the church claims to be "closed" for several hours in the afternoon (Mon-Sat 13:00-17:00, Sun 14:00-17:00), you can still get in by paying €7 (which covers admission to the three interior sights). In other words, one way or another you'll pay €7-8 to thoroughly tour the place; however, if you're skipping the three extras inside, aim to visit the church when it's free.

Hours: Cathedral generally open Mon-Fri 8:00-19:30, Sat-Sun 8:00-20:00. Choir open Mon-Sat 9:00-19:00, closed Sun afternoons. Terrace open Mon-Sat 9:00-18:00, closed Sun. Museum open daily 10:00-19:00, closed Sun. Choir, terrace, and museum may close earlier on slow days.

Dress Code: The dress code is strictly enforced; don't wear tank tops, shorts, or skirts above the knee.

Getting There: The huge, can't-miss-it cathedral is in the center of the Barri Gòtic on Plaça de la Seu (Metro: Jaume I). To get here from Plaça de Catalunya, consider my ✪ Barri Gòtic Walk.

Getting In: The main, front door is open most of the time. While it can be crowded, the line generally moves fast. Sometimes you can enter directly into the cloister (through the door facing the Martyrs statue on the small square along Carrer del Bisbe) or through the side door (facing the Frederic Marès Museum along Carrer dels Comtes).

Information: Tel. 933-151-554, www.catedralbcn.org.

Length of This Tour: Allow 30 minutes, not counting the optional sights (choir, view terrace, museum). With limited time, zip past the many side chapels, but be sure to linger in the cloister.

Services: A tiny, semi-private WC is in the cloister.

Photography: Allowed without a flash.

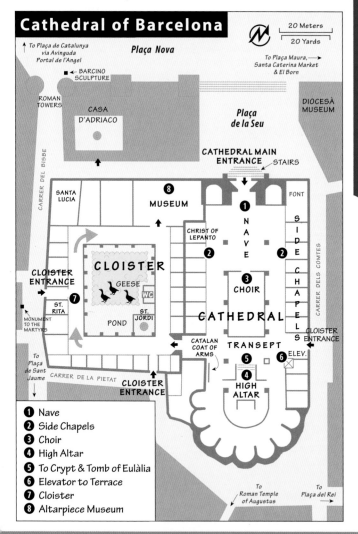

Cathedral of Barcelona

20 Meters
20 Yards

To Plaça de Catalunya
via Avinguda
Portal de l'Angel

Plaça Nova

To Plaça Maura,
Santa Caterina Market
& El Born

BARCINO
SCULPTURE

ROMAN
TOWERS

CASA
D'ADRIACO

Plaça
de la Seu

DIOCESÀ
MUSEUM

CATHEDRAL MAIN
ENTRANCE — STAIRS

CARRER DEL BISBE

SANTA
LUCIA

FONT

MUSEUM ❽

❶ N A V E

S I D E C H A P E L S

CHRIST OF
LEPANTO ❷

❷

CLOISTER
ENTRANCE

CLOISTER

GEESE

WC

❸
CHOIR

CARRER DELS COMTES

❼ ST.
RITA

ST.
JORDI

C A T H E D R A L

CLOISTER
ENTRANCE

MONUMENT
TO THE
MARTYRS

POND

CATALAN
COAT OF
ARMS

TRANSEPT

To
Plaça
de Sant
Jaume

CARRER DE LA PIETAT

CLOISTER
ENTRANCE

❺ ❻ ELEV.

❹
HIGH
ALTAR

❶ Nave

❷ Side Chapels

❸ Choir

❹ High Altar

❺ To Crypt & Tomb of Eulàlia

❻ Elevator to Terrace

❼ Cloister

❽ Altarpiece Museum

To
Roman Temple
of Augustus

To
Plaça del Rei

THE TOUR BEGINS

This has been Barcelona's holiest spot for 2,000 years. The Romans built their Temple of Jupiter here. In A.D. 343, the pagan temple was replaced with a Christian cathedral. That building was supplanted by a Romanesque-style church (11th century). The current Gothic structure was started in 1298 and finished in 1450, during the medieval glory days of the Catalan nation. The facade was humble, so in the 19th century the proud local bourgeoisie (enjoying a second Golden Age) redid it in an ornate, Neo-Gothic style. Construction was capped in 1913 with the central spire, 230 feet tall.

▶ *Enter the main door and take it all in.*

❶ The Nave

The spacious church is 300 feet long and 130 feet wide. Tall pillars made of stone blocks support the crisscross vaults. Each round keystone where the arches cross features a different saint. Typical of many Spanish churches, there's a choir—an enclosed area of wooden seats in the middle

The cathedral, built in medieval times on an ancient site, features soaring arches in the nave.

of the nave, creating a more intimate space for worship. The Gothic church also has fine stained glass, ironwork chandeliers, a 16th-century organ (left transept), tombstones in the pavement, and an "ambulatory" floor plan, allowing worshippers to amble around to the chapel of their choice.

❷ Side Chapels

The nave is ringed with 28 chapels. Besides being worship spaces, these serve as interior buttresses supporting the roof (which is why the exterior walls are smooth, without the normal Gothic buttresses outside). Barcelona honors many of the homegrown saints found in these chapels with public holidays.

From the 13th to 15th century, these side chapels were moneymakers for the church—rented out to guilds to house their business offices. Notice how the iron gates are more than decorative—they also protected the goods and cash inside. The rich ornamentation was sponsored by local guilds as a kind of advertising, here in the community's most high-profile space.

The Church is still fund-raising. The electronic candles that power your prayers cost €0.10 each. (A €0.50 coin lights five.)

▶ *Browse a few chapels, starting in the back-left corner (over your left shoulder as you enter the main door).*

The chapel at the back corner has an old **baptismal font** that once stood in the original fourth-century church. The Native Americans that Columbus brought to town were supposedly baptized here.

▶ *Work your way down the left aisle.*

The first chapel along the left wall is dedicated to **St. Severus,** the bishop here way back in A.D. 290. The second chapel was by, for, and of the local **shoe guild.** Notice the two painted doors with shoes above them that lead to the back office. As the patron of shoemakers was St. Mark, there are plenty of winged lions in this chapel.

▶ *Backtrack a bit, to the large chapel in the back-right corner.*

This chapel (reserved for worship) features the beloved **"Christ of Lepanto"** crucifix. They say the angular wooden figure of Christ leaned to dodge a cannonball during the history-changing Battle of Lepanto (1571), which stopped the Ottomans (and Islam) from advancing into Europe.

▶ *Now head down the right aisle.*

The second chapel has a statue of **St. Anthony** holding the Baby Jesus. His feast day (January 17) is one of many celebrated in the city with an appearance by the *gegants* (giant puppets), a street fair, horse races, and a blessing of pets. The third chapel honors a 20th-century bishop, **San Josep Oriol,** who survived an assassination attempt in the cathedral cloister.

The golden fourth chapel is for **St. Roch** (at the top, pointing to his leg wound, above St. Pancraç), whose feast day is celebrated joyously in the Barri Gòtic in mid-August.

The fifth chapel has a black-and-white sideways statue of **St. Ramon (Raymond) of Penyafort** (1190-1275), the Dominican Bishop of Barcelona who heard Pope Gregory IX's sins and is the patron saint of lawyers (and, therefore, extremely busy). Ramon figures into the city's biggest festival, La Mercè, since he had a miraculous vision of the Virgin of Mercy.

The eighth chapel is worth a look for its over-the-top golden altarpiece decor nearly crowding out **Bishop Pacià**—considered one of the church fathers (c. A.D. 310-391).

▶ *If you want to visit the interior of the choir (described next), pay the fee or show your ticket at the choir entrance (straight ahead from the church's main doors). Otherwise, you can circle around to the far end and peer through the barrier.*

❸ Choir

The 15th-century choir *(coro)* features ornately carved stalls. During the standing parts of the Mass, the chairs were folded up, but VIPs still had those little wooden ledges to lean on. Each was creatively carved and—since you couldn't sit on sacred things—the artists were free to enjoy some secular and naughty fun here.

The choir, lined with carved wood stalls

Twin coffins of Cathedral benefactors

Beneath the high altar, stairs lead down to the tomb of the church's patron saint, Eulàlia.

In 1518, the stalls were painted with the coats of arms of Europe's nobility. They gathered here as members of the Knights of the Golden Fleece to honor Charles V, King of Spain, who was making his first trip to the country he ruled. Like a proto-UN, they also discussed how to work together to defend Europe from the Turkish threat. Check out the detail work on the impressive wood-carved pulpit near the altar, supported by flying angels.

▶ *At the front of the church stands the...*

❹ High Altar

Look behind the altar (beneath the crucifix) to find the bishop's chair, or *cathedra.* As a cathedral, this church is the archbishop's seat—hence its Catalan nickname of *La Seu.* To the left of the altar is the organ and the elevator up to the terrace. To the right of the altar, the wall is decorated with Catalunya's yellow-and-red coat of arms. Under that, the two wooden coffins on the wall are of two powerful Counts of Barcelona (Ramon Berenguer I and his third wife, Almodis), who ordered the construction of the 11th-century Romanesque cathedral that preceded this structure.

▶ *Descend the steps beneath the altar, into the crypt, to see the...*

❺ Tomb of Eulàlia

The marble-and-alabaster sarcophagus (1327-1339) contains the remains of St. Eulàlia. The cathedral is dedicated to this saint. Thirteen-year-old Eulàlia, daughter of a prominent Barcelona family, was martyred by the Romans for her faith in A.D. 304. Murky legends say she was subjected to 13 tortures. First she was stripped naked and had her head shaved, though a miraculous snowfall hid her nakedness. Then she was rolled down the street in a barrel full of sharp objects. After further torments failed to kill her, she was crucified on an X-shaped cross—a symbol you'll find carved into pews and seen throughout the church.

The relief on the coffin's side tells her story in three episodes: She preaches Christianity to the pagan Roman ruler; he orders her to die (while she pleads for mercy); and she's crucified on the X-shaped cross. As one of Barcelona's patron saints, Eulàlia is honored with a festival (with *gegants,* fireworks, and human towers) in mid-February.

▶ *The* ❻ *elevator in the left transept takes you up to the rooftop* **terrace,** *made of sturdy scaffolding pieces, for an expansive city view (ticket required).*

Eulàlia's tomb, carved with her legends

Cloister geese—3 of the chosen 13

Otherwise, head to the right transept and go through the door to enter the...

❼ Cloister

Emerge into the circa-1450 cloister—an arcaded walkway surrounding a lush courtyard. Ahhhh. It's a tropical atmosphere of palm, orange, and magnolia trees, along with a fishpond, trickling fountains, and squawking geese.

From within the cloister, look back at the **arch** you just came through, an impressive mix of Romanesque (arches with chevrons, from the earlier church) and Gothic (pointy top).

The nearby **fountain** has a tiny statue of St. Jordi (George) slaying the dragon. Jordi is one of the patron saints of Catalunya and by far the most popular boy's name here. During the Corpus Christi festival in June, kids come here to watch a hollow egg dance atop the fountain's spray.

As you wander the cloister (clockwise), check out the **coats of arms** as well as the **tombs** in the pavement. These were rich merchants who paid good money to be buried as close to the altar as possible. Notice the symbols of their trades: scissors, shoes, bakers, and so on. The cloister had a practical, economic purpose. The church sold out all its chapel space, and this opened up an entire new wing to donors. A second floor was planned (look up) but not finished.

The resident **geese** have been here for at least 500 years. There are always 13, in memory of Eulàlia's 13 years and 13 torments. Other legends say they're white as a symbol of her virginity. Before modern security systems, they acted as alarms, honking to alert the monk in charge. Faithful to tradition, they honk to this very day.

Farther along the cloister, next to the door, the **Chapel of Santa Rita** (patron saint of impossible causes) usually has the most candles. In the next corner of the cloister is the barrel-vaulted **Chapel of Santa Lucía,** a small 13th-century remnant of the earlier Romanesque cathedral. It's quite dark, as churches were before the advent of Gothic style. People hoping for good eyesight (Santa Lucía's specialty) pray here. Notice the nice eyes in the modern restoration of the altar painting.

▶ At the far end of the cloister, you'll find the...

❽ Altarpiece Museum (Museu Capitular)

The little museum has the six-foot-tall 14th-century Great Monstrance, a ceremonial display case for the communion wafer. Made of gold and studded with jewels, it's really three separate parts: a church-like central section, topped with a crown canopy, standing on a golden chair. This huge monstrance with its wafer is paraded through the streets during the Corpus Christi festival. Nearby is a gold-plated silver statue of St. Eulàlia, carrying the X-shaped cross she was crucified on. An 11th-century baptismal font from the Romanesque church is also on view.

The next room, the Sala Capitular, has several altarpieces, including a *pietá* (a.k.a. *Desplà*) by Bartolomé Bermejo (1490). An anguished Mary cradles a twisted Christ against a bleak, stormy landscape. It's unique in Spanish art for its Italianesque, Renaissance 3-D. Rather than your basic gold backdrop, this has a strong foreground (the mourners), middle distance (the cross), and background (the city and distant hills). The kneeling donors who paid for the painting are photorealistic, complete with reading glasses and five o'clock shadows.

▶ Our tour is over. May peace be with you.

Picasso Museum Tour

Museu Picasso

This is the best collection in the country of the work of Spaniard Pablo Picasso (1881-1973). And, since Picasso spent his formative years (from ages 14 to 23) in Barcelona, it's the best collection of his early works anywhere. The museum is sparse on later, better-known works from his time of international celebrity; visit not to see famous canvases but to get an intimate portrait of the young man finding his way as an artist. By experiencing his youthful, realistic art, you can better understand his later, more challenging art and more fully appreciate his genius.

The artist himself donated pieces to the museum in his later life, happy to have a place showing off his work in the city of his youth.

ORIENTATION

Cost: €11-14 for timed-entry ticket, free all day first Sun of month and other Sun from 15:00.

Hours: Tue-Sun 9:00-19:00, Thu until 21:30, closed Mon.

Crowd-Avoiding Tips: There's almost always a line, sometimes with waits over an hour. During peak season, it's possible that tickets, which include an entry time, may sell out. Advance tickets sold via the museum website guarantee an entry time with no wait (no booking fee, www.museupicasso.bcn.cat). Or, if you have an Articket BCN or plan to buy one (✪ see page 170), skip the line by going to the "Meeting Point" entry (30 yards to the right of the main entry). To buy day-of tickets, go early and check the screen near the ticket office for availability. The museum's busiest times are mornings before 13:00, all day Tue, and during the free entry times on Sun.

Getting There: It's at Carrer de Montcada 15; the ticket office is at #21. From the Jaume I Metro stop, head down Carrer de la Princesa (across busy Via Laietana from the Barri Gòtic), turning right on Carrer de Montcada.

Information: Tel. 932-563-000, www.museupicasso.bcn.cat.

Tours: The 1.5-hour audioguide (€5) offers ample detail.

Length of This Tour: Allow at least an hour.

Services: The ground floor, which is free to enter, has a required bag check, bookshop, WC, and cafeteria.

Photography: Strictly forbidden.

Cuisine Art: Near the museum, along Carrer de Montcada, are several recommended tapas bars: El Xampanyet, Taverna Tapeo, and Bar del Pla.

Picasso Museum—First Floor

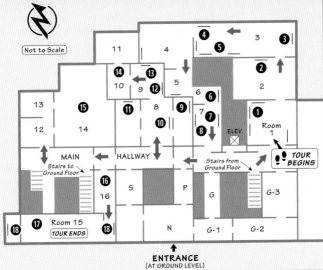

Not to Scale

4 ← 3 **3**
11 4 **5**
  2
14 **13** 2
10 9 **12**
15 **11** 6 **6**
13 8 **9**
12 14 7 **7**
  10 8 **1** ELEV. ☒ Room 1
  👣 **TOUR BEGINS**
MAIN ← HALLWAY *Stairs from Ground Floor*
Stairs to Ground Floor
  16 S P G G-3
  16
18 **17** Room 15 **18** N G-1 G-2
  TOUR ENDS

ENTRANCE
(AT GROUND LEVEL)
CARRER DE MONTCADA

← To Santa Caterina Market
(5 min. walk)

To Church of Santa Maria del Mar →
(5 min. walk)

To Jaume 1 Ⓜ (5 min. walk)
& Cathedral (10 min. walk)

1 Portraits &
Art-School Work

2 First Communion

3 Science and Charity

4 Velázquez Copy

5 Horta de San Joan

6 Cancan Dancer

7 Still Life

8 The Waiting (Margot)

9 Motherhood

10 Rooftops of Barcelona

11 Portrait of Bernadetta
Bianco

12 Woman with Mantilla

13 Gored Horse

14 Synthetic Cubism

15 Las Meninas Studies

16 Ceramics

17 French Riviera

18 Portraits of Jacqueline (2)

THE TOUR BEGINS

The Picasso Museum's collection of nearly 300 paintings is presented more or less chronologically. The art is scattered through several connected Gothic palaces. Be aware that specific pieces may be out for restoration or on tour, and the rooms are rearranged every few months or so. But with the help of thoughtful English descriptions for each stage (and guards who don't let you stray), it's easy to follow the evolution of Picasso's life and work.

▶ *Begin in Rooms 1 and 2.*

Boy Wonder

Pablo's earliest art (in the first room) is realistic and earnest. His work quickly advances from childish pencil drawings from about 1890, through a series of technically skilled art-school works (copies of plaster feet and arms), to oil paintings of impressive technique.

Even at a young age, his **portraits** of grizzled peasants demonstrate surprising psychological insight. Because his dedicated father—himself a curator and artist—kept everything his son ever did, Picasso must have the best-documented youth of any great painter.

▶ *In Room 2, you'll find more paintings relating to Pablo's...*

Developing Talent

During a summer trip to Málaga in 1896, Picasso dabbles in a series of fresh, Impressionistic-style landscapes (relatively rare in Spain at the time). As a 15-year-old, Pablo dutifully enters art-school competitions. His first big work, ***First Communion*** (1896), features a prescribed religious subject, but Picasso makes it an excuse to paint his family. His sister Lola is the model for the communicant, and the features of the man beside her belong to Picasso's father. Notice Lola's exquisitely painted veil. This piece is heavily influenced by the academic style of local painters.

Picasso's relatives star in a number of portraits from this time. If it's on view, find the **portrait of his mother** (this and other family portraits are among those frequently rotated). The teenage Pablo is working on the fine details and gradients of white in her blouse and the expression in her cameo-like face. Notice the signature. Spaniards keep both parents' surnames, with the father's first, followed by the mother's: Pablo Ruiz Picasso.

▶ *Continue into Room 3.*

Early Success

Science and Charity (1897), which won second prize at a fine-arts exhibition, got Picasso the chance to study in Madrid. Now Picasso conveys real feeling. The doctor (modeled on Pablo's father) represents science. The nun represents charity and religion. From her hopeless face and lifeless hand, it seems that Picasso believes nothing will save this woman from death. Pablo painted a little perspective trick: Walk back and forth across the room to see the bed stretch and shrink. Three small studies for this painting (on the right) show how this was an exploratory work. The frontier: light.

Picasso travels to Madrid for further study. Stifled by the stuffy fine-arts school there, he hangs out instead in the Prado Museum and learns by copying the masters. An example of his impressive mimicry is at the end of this room. Notice young Picasso's nearly perfect copy of a **portrait of Philip IV** by an earlier Spanish master, Diego Velázquez. (Near the end of this tour, we'll see a much older Picasso riffing on another Velázquez painting.) Having absorbed the wisdom of the ages, in 1898 Pablo visits **Horta**

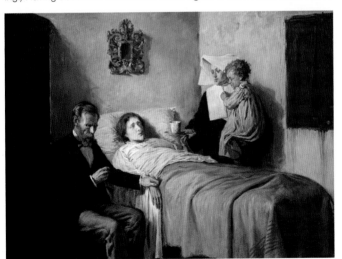

Science and Charity—The 16-year-old son of an art teacher wowed Spain with his mature insight.

de San Joan, a rural Catalan village, and finds his artistic independence. (See the small landscapes and scenes of village life he did there.) Poor and without a love in his life, he returns to Barcelona.

▶ *Head to Room 4.*

Barcelona Freedom

Art Nouveau is all the rage in Barcelona when Pablo returns there in 1900. Upsetting his dad, he quits art school and falls in with the avant-garde crowd. These bohemians congregate daily at Els Quatre Gats ("The Four Cats," a popular restaurant to this day—✪ see page 40). Picasso even created the **menu cover** for this favorite hangout (it's sometimes on view here in Room 4). Further establishing his artistic freedom, he paints **portraits** of his new friends (including one of Jaume Sabartés, who later became his personal assistant and donated the works to establish this museum). Only 19 years old, Pablo puts on his first one-man show at Els Quatre Gats in 1900.

▶ *Continue through Room 5. The next few pieces are displayed in Rooms 6 and 7.*

Paris

In 1900 Picasso makes his first trip to Paris, a city bursting with life, light, and love. Dropping the paternal surname Ruiz, Pablo establishes his commercial brand name: "Picasso." Here the explorer Picasso goes bohemian and befriends poets, prostitutes, and artists. He paints **cancan dancers** like Henri de Toulouse-Lautrec, **still lifes** like Paul Cézanne, brightly colored Fauvist works like Henri Matisse, and Impressionist **landscapes** like Claude Monet. In *The Waiting (Margot),* the subject—with her bold outline and strong gaze—pops out from the vivid, mosaic-like background. It is Cézanne's technique of "building" a figure with "cubes" of paint that will inspire Picasso to invent Cubism—soon.

▶ *Turn right into the hall, then—farther along—right again, to find Rooms 8 and 9.*

Blue Period

Picasso travels to Paris several times (he settles there permanently in 1904). The suicide of his best friend, his own poverty, and the influence of new ideas linking color and mood lead Picasso to abandon jewel-bright color for his Blue Period (1901-1904). He cranks out stacks of blue art just

Picasso painted still lifes like Cezanne, later crystallizing the geometric shapes into Cubism.

to stay housed and fed. With blue backgrounds (the coldest color) and depressing subjects, this period was revolutionary in art history. Now the artist is painting not what he sees, but what he feels. Just off Room 8, look for the touching 1903 portrait of a mother and child, **Motherhood** (this very fragile pastel is only displayed intermittently), which captures the period well. Painting misfits and street people, Picasso, like Velázquez and Toulouse-Lautrec, sees the beauty in ugliness. Back home in Barcelona, Picasso paints his hometown at night from **rooftops** (in the main part of Room 8). The painting is still blue, but here we see proto-Cubism...five years before the first real Cubist painting.

▶ In the left section of Room 8, we get a hint of Picasso's...

Rose Period

Picasso is finally lifted out of his funk after meeting a new lady, Fernande Olivier. He moves out of the blue and into the happier Rose Period (1904-1907). For a fine example, see the portrait of a woman wearing a classic Spanish mantilla **(Portrait of Bernadetta Bianco).** Its soft pink and

The Life of Pablo Picasso (1881-1973)

Pablo Picasso was the most famous and, for me, the greatest artist of the 20th century. Always exploring, he became the master of many styles (Cubism, Surrealism, Expressionism, and so on) and of many media (painting, sculpture, prints, ceramics, and assemblages). Still, he could make anything he touched look unmistakably like "a Picasso."

Born in Málaga, Spain, Picasso was the son of an art teacher. At a very young age, he quickly advanced beyond his teachers. Picasso's teenage works are stunningly realistic and capture the inner complexities of the people he painted. As a youth in Barcelona, he fell in with a bohemian crowd that mixed wine, women, and art.

In 1900, at age 19, Picasso started making trips to Paris. Four years later, he moved to the City of Light and absorbed the styles of many painters (especially Henri de Toulouse-Lautrec) while searching for his own artist's voice. His paintings of beggars and other social outcasts show the empathy of a man who was himself a poor, homesick foreigner. When his best friend, Spanish artist Carlos Casagemas, committed suicide, Picasso plunged into a **Blue Period** (1901-1904)—so called because the dominant color in these paintings matches their melancholy mood and subject matter (emaciated beggars, hard-eyed pimps, and so on).

In 1904, Picasso got a steady girl-friend (Fernande Olivier) and suddenly saw the world through rose-colored glasses—the **Rose Period.** He was further jolted out of his Blue Period by the "flat" look of the Fauves. Not satisfied with their take on 3-D, Picasso played with the "building blocks" of line and color to find new ways to reconstruct the real world on canvas.

At his studio in Montmartre, Picasso and his neighbor Georges Braque worked together, in poverty so dire they often didn't know where their next bottle of wine was coming from. And then, at the age of 25, Picasso reinvented painting. Fascinated by the primitive power of African and Iberian tribal masks, he sketched human faces with simple outlines and almond eyes. Intrigued by the body of his girlfriend, Fernande, he sketched it from every angle, and then experimented with showing several different views on the same canvas. A hundred paintings and nine months later, Picasso gave birth to a monstrous canvas of five nude, fragmented prostitutes with mask-like faces—*Les Demoiselles d'Avignon* (1907). (The painting's name came not from the French city but from the once-brothel-lined Carrer d'Avinyo in Barcelona's Barri Gòtic.)

This bold new style was called **Cubism.** With Cubism, Picasso shattered the Old World and put it back together in a new way. The subjects are somewhat recognizable (with the help of the titles), but they're built with geometric shards (let's call them "cubes")—like viewing the world through a kaleidoscope of brown and gray. Cubism gives us several different angles of the subject at once—say, a woman seen from the front and side angles simultaneously, resulting in two eyes on the same side of the nose. This involves showing the traditional three dimensions, plus Einstein's new fourth dimension—the time it takes to walk around the subject to see other angles.

In 1918, Picasso married his first wife, Olga Kokhlova, with whom he had a son. He then traveled to Rome and entered a **Classical Period** (the 1920s) of more realistic, full-bodied women and children, inspired by the three-dimensional sturdiness of ancient statues. While he flirted with abstraction, throughout his life, Picasso always kept a grip on "reality." His favorite subject was people. The anatomy might be jumbled, but it's all there.

Though he lived in France and Italy, Picasso remained a Spaniard at heart, incorporating Spanish motifs into his work. Unrepentantly macho, he loved bullfights, seeing them as a metaphor for the timeless human interaction between the genders. The horse—clad with blinders

continued on next page

The Life of Pablo Picasso cont'd from previous page

and pummeled by the bull—is just a pawn in the battle between bull and matador. To Picasso, the horse symbolizes the feminine, and the bull, the masculine. Spanish imagery—bulls, screaming horses, a Madonna—appears in Picasso's most famous work, *Guernica* (1937, on display in Madrid). The monumental canvas of a bombed village summed up the pain of Spain's brutal civil war (1936-1939) and foreshadowed the onslaught of World War II.

At war's end, Picasso left Paris, his wife, and his emotional baggage behind, finding fun in the sun in the **south of France.** Sun! Color! Water! Spacious skies! Freedom! Senior citizen Pablo Picasso was reborn, enjoying worldwide fame. He lived at first with the beautiful young painter Françoise Gilot, mother of two of his children, but soon replaced her with another young beauty, Jacqueline Roque, who became his second wife. Dressed in rolled-up white pants and a striped sailor's shirt, bursting with pent-up creativity, Picasso often cranked out a painting a day. Picasso's Riviera works set the tone for the rest of his life—sunny, lighthearted, uncomplicated, experimenting in new media and using motifs of the sea, of Greek mythology (fauns, centaurs), and animals (birds, goats, and pregnant baboons). His simple drawing of doves became an international symbol of peace.

Picasso also made collages, built "statues" out of wood, wire, ceramics, papier-mâché, or whatever, and even turned everyday household objects into statues (like his famous bull's head made of a bicycle seat with handlebar horns). **Multimedia** works like these have become so standard today that we forget how revolutionary they were when Picasso invented them. His last works have the playfulness of someone much younger. As it is often said of Picasso, "When he was a child, he painted like a man. When he was old, he painted like a child."

reddish tones are the colors of flesh and sensuality. (This is the only actual Rose Period painting in the museum, but don't be surprised if it is "sleeping" or out on loan.)

Barcelona

Picasso spent six months back in Barcelona in 1917 (his girlfriend, a Russian ballet dancer, had a gig in town). The paintings in these rooms demonstrate the artist's irrepressible versatility: He's already developed Cubism (with his friend Georges Braque; more on this below), but he also continues to play with other styles. In **Woman with Mantilla** (Room 9), we

Woman with Mantilla—Even after he moved to Paris, Picasso used motifs from his native land.

see a little Post-Impressionistic Pointillism in a portrait that is as elegant as a classical statue. Nearby, **Gored Horse** has all the anguish and power of his iconic *Guernica* (painted years later).

▶ *Continue through room 10, into room 11.*

Cubism

Pablo's invention (roughly from 1906 to 1913, with fellow artist Georges Braque) of the revolutionary Cubist style is well-known—at least I hope so, since this museum has no true Cubist paintings. Cubist work gives not only the basics of a subject—it shows every aspect of it simultaneously. In this museum, you'll see some so-called **Synthetic Cubist paintings** (Room 10)—a later variation that flattens the various angles, as opposed to the purer, original Analytical Cubist paintings, in which you can simultaneously see several 3-D facets of the subject.

▶ *Remember that this museum focuses on Picasso's early years, with very little from the most famous and prolific "middle" part of his career—from Picasso's adoption of Cubism to his sunset years on the French Riviera. Skip ahead more than 30 years and into Rooms 12-14 (at the end of the main hallway, on the right).*

Picasso and Velázquez

A series of Picasso's works relates to what many consider the greatest painting by anyone, ever: Diego Velázquez's *Las Meninas* (the 17th-century original is displayed in Madrid's Prado Museum). Heralded as the first completely realistic painting, *Las Meninas* became an obsession for Picasso centuries later.

Picasso, who had great respect for Velázquez, painted more than **40 interpretations** of this piece. Picasso seems to enjoy a relationship of equals with Velázquez. Like artistic soul mates, the two Spanish geniuses spar and tease. Picasso deconstructs Velázquez and then injects light, color, and perspective as he improvises on the earlier masterpiece. In Picasso's big black-and-white canvas, the king and queen (reflected in the mirror in the back of the room) are hardly seen, while the painter towers above everyone. The two women of the court on the right look like they're in a tomb—but they're wearing party shoes. Browse the various studies, a playground of color and perspective. See the fun Picasso had playing paddleball with Velázquez's tour de force—filtering Velázquez's realism through the kaleidoscope of Cubism.

Synthetic Cubism

Picasso improvised off the master Velázquez.

▶ *Head back down the hall and turn right, through the* **ceramics** *area (Room 16), to find a flock of carefree white birds in Room 15. Enjoy the palace decoration as it looked before the building became a museum.*

The French Riviera (Last Years)

Picasso spends the last 36 years of his life living simply in the south of France. He said many times that "Paintings are like windows open to the world." We see his sunny Riviera world: With simple black outlines and Crayola colors, Picasso paints sun-splashed nature, peaceful doves, and the joys of the beach. He dabbles in the timeless art of ceramics, shaping bowls and vases into fun animals decorated with simple, childlike designs. He's enjoying life with his second (and much younger) wife, Jacqueline Roque, whose portraits hang nearby.

Picasso died with brush in hand, still growing. Sadly, since Picasso vowed never to set foot in a fascist, Franco-ruled Spain, the artist never returned to his homeland...and never saw this museum (his death came in 1973—two years before Franco's). However, to the end, Picasso continued exploring and loving life through his art.

▶ *Our tour is finished. You're in the heart of the delightful El Born neighborhood. To explore this area further,* ✪ *see my El Born Walk on page 114.*

Eixample Walk

From Plaça de Catalunya to La Pedrera (and Beyond)

Literally "The Expansion," L'Eixample is where Barcelona spread when it burst at the seams in the 19th century. City planners created a refreshingly open grid plan of broad, straight boulevards—the opposite of the claustrophobic Gothic lanes that had contained locals for centuries. In the mid-1800s, Barcelona was humming. The Eixample reflects two important historic movements: the revival of Catalan cultural pride (the Renaixença), and the emergence of Catalunya's own spin on Art Nouveau (Modernisme). It was a perfect storm of urban planning, architectural innovation, Industrial Age technology, ample wealth, and Catalan pride.

 The core of this walk is two of the city's Modernista musts—the Block of Discord and La Pedrera (Casa Milà). We'll also wind through some untouristy residential areas that showcase the vibrant vibe of Barcelona today.

ORIENTATION

Length of This Walk: Allow 1.5 hours—more if you tour the sights.

Reservations: To see the interiors, reservations are essential for Casa Lleó Morera. Advance purchase is smart for Casa Batlló, Casa Amatller, and La Pedrera.

Getting There: Start at Plaça de Catalunya (Metro: Plaça de Catalunya).

When to Go: By day, you can visit the interiors of La Pedrera, Casa Batlló, Casa Amatller, the Church of the Holy Conception (closes for mid-afternoon siesta), the Fundació Antoni Tàpies (closed Mon), and La Concepció Market (closed Sun). At night, the interiors are closed, but you can still see floodlit facades and enjoy the lively tapas bar scene.

Casa Batlló: €21.50, daily 9:00-21:00, advance ticket info on ✪ page 120.

Casa Amatller: €15 guided tour, daily 11:00-18:00, advance ticket info on ✪ page 120.

Casa Lleó Morera: €15 for 70-minute English tour, reservation info on ✪ page 121.

La Pedrera (Casa Milà): €20.50, daily March-Oct 9:00-20:00, Nov-Feb 9:00-18:30, last entry 30 minutes before closing, ticket info and crowd-beating tips on ✪ page 122.

Eating: Several fine tapas bars and restaurants are nearby. For details, ✪ see page 152.

Background

Barcelona boomed in the 1800s, with its population doubling (from a half-million to a million) over the course of one century. Before its roaring 19th century, Barcelona languished through centuries of stagnation: Columbus' discoveries had shifted trade from the Mediterranean to

the Atlantic. Catalunya also suffered under the thumb of Madrid, which feared—perhaps rightfully—a Catalan uprising.

Eventually the Spanish Queen Isabella II loosened Madrid's grip on Barcelona. This land of abundant coal deposits and many rivers flowing from the Pyrenees to the Mediterranean provided the perfect resources for powering textile mills. Industrialization brought workers from all over Spain (and beyond). Barcelona was back on the map.

But the upwardly mobile city had nowhere to grow. Because of the Madrid government's centuries-old restrictions, the city was forced to stay within its medieval walls. By the mid-19th century, 200,000 residents were crammed into the Old City. It was a slum of steep and crowded tenements, where disease was rampant and the quality of life was miserable. It was clear that expansion was necessary.

Throughout Europe in the Industrial Age, cities like Paris, Vienna, and Copenhagen were dealing with similar growing pains: dense population and squalor needlessly corralled into tight quarters by antiquated defensive city walls. In 1854, Queen Isabella II allowed Barcelona to tear down the medieval wall and expand northward. Because very little existed outside the Old City, urban planners had a blank slate.

Civil engineer Ildefons Cerdà (1815-1876) created a remarkably modern and efficient grid of streets, but with a people-friendly twist: By snipping off the building corners, light and spacious octagonal "squares" were created at every intersection. Each block-square district would have easy access to its own hospital, park, market, schools, and day-care centers. Strict zoning codes made sure sunlight would reach every unit. The hollow space inside each "block" of apartments would form a neighborhood park. The Eixample was a modern marvel of urban planning. Rich-and-artsy big shots gobbled up this prime real estate, especially along the main drag, Passeig de Gràcia. They built mansions to show off their wealth and status, hiring the best and brightest architects in the business (✪ see the sidebar on page 86).

Today's Eixample is still the city's most desirable neighborhood. It's also one center of the local gay community (especially around Carrer d'Aribau), earning it the nickname "Gayshample." The heart of the Eixample is the Quadrat d'Or, or "Golden Quarter," with the richest collection of Modernista facades...and the richest local residents.

Modernisme and the Renaixença

Modernisme is Barcelona's unique contribution to the Europe-wide Art Nouveau movement. Meaning "a taste for what is modern"—things like streetcars, electric lights, and big-wheeled bicycles—this free-flowing organic style lasted from 1888 to 1906.

The starting point for the style was a kind of Neo-Gothic, clearly inspired by medieval castles, towers, and symbols—logically, since architects wanted to recall Barcelona's glory days of the 1400s when it ruled a shipping empire. From the Neo-Gothic look, Antoni Gaudí branched off on his own, adding the color and curves we most associate with Barcelona's Modernisme look.

The aim was to create objects that were both practical and decorative. Modernista architects experimented with new construction techniques, especially concrete, which they could use to make a hard stone building that curved and rippled like a wave. Then they sprinkled it with brightly colored glass and tile. The structure was fully modern, but the decoration was a clip-art collage of nature images, exotic Moorish or Chinese themes, and fanciful Gothic crosses and knights to celebrate Catalunya's medieval glory days.

Modernisme was a response against the regimentation of the Industrial Age—but all those organic shapes were only made possible thanks to Eiffel Tower-like iron frames. The Eixample's fanciful facades and colorful, leafy ornamentation were built at the same time as the first skyscrapers in Chicago and New York City.

Underpinning Modernisme was the Catalan cultural revival movement, called the Renaixença. Across Europe, it was a time of national resurgence. It was the dawn of the modern age, and downtrodden peoples—from the Basques to the Irish to the Hungarians to the Finns—were throwing off the cultural domination of other nations and celebrating what made their own cultures unique. Here in Catalunya, the Renaixença encouraged everyday people to get excited about all things Catalan—from their language, patriotic dances, and inspirational art to their surprising style of architecture.

THE WALK BEGINS

▶ *Begin at Plaça de Catalunya. Head up the broad boulevard (Passeig de Gràcia) at the top end of the giant El Corte Inglés department store. Walk two blocks (on the right side of this street) to the huge intersection with Gran Via de les Corts Catalanes; there's a big fountain in the middle.*

❶ Passeig de Gràcia

In the 500 feet between here and the Barri Gòtic, you've traveled 500 years—from the medieval Gothic vibe of the Barri Gòtic to the ambitiously modern late-19th-century Eixample.

In Catalan, *passeig* means "boulevard"—and this one leads to Gràcia, once a separate town but now overwhelmed by Barcelona's growth and a neighborhood within the city. As one of the first major thoroughfares of the Eixample, this was prime real estate. Barcelona's richest built their mansions here, as close as possible to Plaça de Catalunya. (One of the few surviving mansions, now the Comedia theater, is kitty-corner across the intersection—just beyond the fountain.) To this day, it's the top street

Plaça de Catalunya—dividing old and new Barcelona—marks the start of stately Passeig de Gràcia.

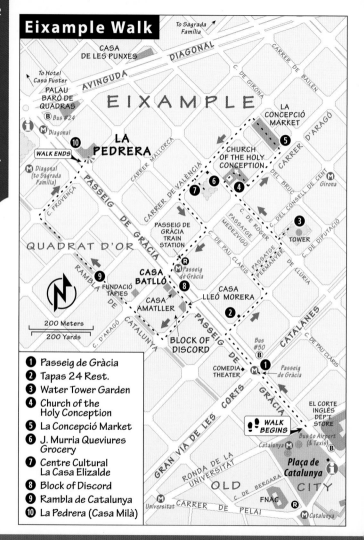

Eixample Walk

1 Passeig de Gràcia
2 Tapas 24 Rest.
3 Water Tower Garden
4 Church of the Holy Conception
5 La Concepció Market
6 J. Murria Queviures Grocery
7 Centre Cultural La Casa Elizalde
8 Block of Discord
9 Rambla de Catalunya
10 La Pedrera (Casa Milà)

in town. Notice the extra-wide girth, the inviting park-like median strips, and the unique Modernista lampposts anchored by Gaudí-style benches slathered with broken white tile mosaics.

Despite their varied facades, most Eixample homes share an identical design: The entire building was owned by one family that lived in the middle and rented space above and below. Shops and businesses were on the ground floor; above that, a large first (our "second") floor where the wealthy family lived; and higher up, smaller floors for tenants. The first floor is usually more elaborate than the other floors—often with balconies or bay windows that higher floors are lacking. (Most of these houses predate the elevator; after that convenience was invented and widely installed, penthouse living became popular.) Many houses have two doors—one for the owners, and another for the upstairs tenants. Most house blocks had an interior garden courtyard for ventilation and light, although over time many of these spaces have been covered over by one-story structures or parking lots.

Because the Eixample was developed during the Renaixença, you'll spot Catalan themes, such as St. George (Jordi)—the local patron saint—slaying the dragon. You might see the Catalunyan flag, with its simple block of narrow red-and-gold stripes. The version with the blue triangle with a white star is a call for independence from Spain inspired by the flag of Cuba (which successfully won its independence from Spain long ago). Speaking of Catalan pride, this street is where massive crowds of Catalans sometimes gather to demonstrate for Catalunyan autonomy. *"Som una nació,"* they chant. *"Nosaltres decidim."* We are a nation. We decide.

Continue to the intersection with Carrer de la Diputació. With its four corners cropped off, the intersection becomes a wide-open, pleasant space for café tables, inviting benches, or public art.

▶ *From here, turn right on Carrer de la Diputació. (If you're tight on time you can continue directly ahead to stop #8 on this walk, the Block of Discord.)*

❷ Tapas 24

A few steps down on the left, you'll see the recommended Tapas 24, a popular and trendy Eixample tapas bar (for more tapas bar listings, ✪ see page 152).

Continue one block down Carrer de la Diputació, noticing the typical tile paving stones (four squares with a circle in each one), which have become a symbol of Barcelona.

▶ *At the corner, cross the street and turn left up Carrer de Pau Claris. Halfway up the block, turn right into the gated* **passage** *(Passatge Permanyer, at #116). Cut through here for a peek at a fine residential strip buried in the middle of the block. Popping out the other end, go right to cross the street and jog 30 yards to the left, then go down the passage at #56 (on the right, marked Jardins de Torre de les Aigües, €1.50, Mon-Sat 10:00-20:00). This leads you to a...*

❸ Water Tower Garden

This tranquil (if somewhat sterile) courtyard has trees, benches, and a wading pool, all watched over by a brick water tower from 1867. In the summer, a temporary "beach" is created here for neighborhood families. Courtyards like this were part of the original vision for the Eixample. But over time, many were converted to other purposes. More recently, the city of Barcelona has slowly begun restoring Cerdà's original public spaces.

▶ *Exiting the garden the way you entered, turn right and head up Carrer de Roger de Llúria. Cross Carrer del Consell de Cent, passing under a pretty yellow Neo-Renaissance facade slapped onto a modern building.*

Continue another block and cross another street (Carrer d'Aragó). Go straight up Carrer de Roger de Llúria a half-block, entering the delightful cloister with orange, magnolia, and palm trees at #70, on the right of the...

❹ Church of the Holy Conception

Work your way through the cloister to the interior of the church. This 13th-century Gothic church once stood in the Old City. But in the 1870s, it was moved, brick by brick, to this spot, to bring a bit of old-time religion to the newly developed Eixample. The bell tower came from a different Gothic church.

▶ *Exiting the church through its front door, turn left, go one block, and cross Carrer del Bruc. On the left is...*

❺ La Concepció Market

Though just as colorful as La Boqueria (on the Ramblas) and the Santa Caterina Market (in El Born), this market (with a modern supermarket in the basement) has virtually zero tourists. Walk through the building, from one end to the other. It's a good place to sample local cheeses, buy olives,

Water Tower Garden's brick tower once provided Eixample residents with running water.

The Stars of Modernisme

Yes, you'll hear plenty about Gaudí, but he's merely one of many great minds who contributed to the architectural revolution of Modernisme. Here's a rundown of the movement's major players. You'll see many of these works along this walk.

Antoni Gaudí (1852-1926), Barcelona's most famous Modernista artist, was descended from four generations of metalworkers—a lineage of which he was quite proud. He incorporated ironwork into his architecture and came up with novel approaches to architectural structure and space. Gaudí's work strongly influenced his younger Catalan contemporary, Salvador Dalí. Notice the similarities: While Dalí was creating unlikely and shocking juxtapositions of photorealistic images, Gaudí did the  same in architecture—using the spine of a reptile for a bannister or a turtle shell design on windows. Entire trips (and lives) are dedicated to seeing the works of Gaudí, but on a brief visit in Barcelona, the ones most worth considering are his great unfinished church, the Sagrada Família; several mansions in the town center, including La Pedrera, Casa Batlló, and Palau Güell; and Park Güell, his ambitious and never-completed housing development.

Lluís Domènech i Montaner (1850-1923), a professor and politician, was responsible for some major civic buildings, including his masterwork, the Palace of Catalan Music (✪ see page 117). He also

or pick up some fruit. At the far end, you'll emerge into a delightful flower market crowding the sidewalk.
▸ *Turn left and walk along...*

Carrer de València

Stroll a few blocks and enjoy some features of everyday life in the Eixample. You'll pass flower stands, the turreted Municipal Conservatory (a music

designed Casa Lleó Morera on the Block of Discord and Casa Fuster (now a luxury hotel).

Josep Puig i Cadafalch (1867-1956) was a city planner who oversaw the opening up of Via Laietana through the middle of the Old City. He was instrumental in the redevelopment of Montjuïc for the 1929 World Expo. As a home builder, he designed Casa de les Punxes and Casa Amatller on the Block of Discord. He also designed the brick factory complex that has been converted into the cutting-edge CaixaForum exhibition space (✪ see page 132). Perhaps most importantly, Puig i Cadafalch designed the building housing Els Quatre Gats (✪ see page 150), a bar that became a cradle of sorts for the whole Modernista movement.

All architects worked with a team of people who, while not famous, made real contributions. For example, Gaudí's colleague **Josep Maria Jujol** (1879-1949) is primarily responsible for much of what Gaudí became known for—the broken-tile mosaic decorations (called *trencadís*) on Park Güell's benches and La Pedrera's chimneys.

Though not an artist, businessman **Eusebi Güell** (1846-1918) is worth a mention. He used his nearly $90 billion fortune to bankroll Gaudí and others, much as the Medici financed Michelangelo and Leonardo da Vinci. Güell's name still adorns two of Gaudí's most important works: Palau Güell and Park Güell (✪ described on pages 110 and 123).

school), an ugly brick monstrosity, and (at #293) a fine Modernista building with wrought-iron railings and twin bay windows. Peek inside ❻ **J. Murria Queviures** (at Carrer de Roger de Llúria 85), a classic Modernista grocery. The vintage ad on the corner—dubbed *La Mona y el Mono (The Classy Lady and the Monkey)*—advertised anise liquor to Modernista-era clients.

Press ahead a half-block farther to the ❼ **Centre Cultural La Casa Elizalde** (at Carrer de València 302, on the left), a hive of city-sponsored classes and activities. Heading down the passage, you'll pop out into an appealing courtyard in the middle of the block with benches. You'll find WCs inside the building: women, first floor; men, second floor.

Ponder the fact that in just a few blocks, we've passed a church, a market, a school, a community center, and an array of shops. This is very much in keeping with the original vision for the Eixample: a series of self-sufficient neighborhood zones that give residents easy access to important services.

▶ *Head back out to the street and turn left (the way you were going). At the end of the block, go left down Carrer de Pau Claris. After a block, turn right on the wide Carrer d'Aragó. Walk one block, stand on the corner, and you'll find yourself kitty-corner from the...*

❽ Block of Discord (Illa de la Discòrdia)

One block, three buildings, three astonishingly creative Modernista architects. Over a short span of time, the three big names of Catalunya's bold Art Nouveau architectural movement erected innovative facades along this one short stretch of Passeig de Gràcia. Although each of these architects has better works elsewhere in town, this is the most convenient place to see their sharply contrasting visions side by side. While these three buildings were done by famous, groundbreaking architects, the whole block is a jumble of delightful architectural whimsy. Reliefs, coats of arms, ironwork, gables, and bay windows adorn otherwise ordinary buildings.

▶ *Work your way down the block, beginning with the unmistakably Gaudí-style facade that's one building in from the corner.*

Casa Batlló (#43)

The most famous facade on the block is that of the green-blue ceramic-speckled Casa Batlló, designed by Antoni Gaudí (you can tour the interior—✪ see listing on page 120). It's thought that Gaudí based the work on the popular legend of St. George (Jordi) slaying the dragon: The humpback roofline suggests a cresting dragon's back, and the smallest, top balcony is shaped like a rosebud (echoing the legend that a rose grew in the place where St. George spilled the dragon's blood). The building's tibia-like pillars and skull-like balconies evoke the dragon's victims. Notice also the random broken tiles, a Gaudí trademark that only later became appreciated. The tiled roof has a soft-ice-cream-cone turret topped with a cross. But some see instead a Mardi Gras theme, with mask-like balconies, a

Gaudí's dragon-spine roof on Casa Batlló

Casa Amatller's step-gable roofline

facade flecked with purple and gold confetti, and the ridge of a harlequin's hat up top. The inscrutable Gaudí preferred to leave his designs open to interpretation.

▶ Next door is...

Casa Amatller (#41)

Josep Puig i Cadafalch completely remodeled this house for the Amatller chocolate-making family. The facade features a creative mix of three of Spain's historical traditions: Moorish-style pentagram-and-vine designs; Gothic-style tracery, gargoyles, and bay windows; and the step-gable roof from Spain's Habsburg connection to the Low Countries. Notice the many layers of the letter "A": The house itself (with its gable) forms an A, as does the decorative frieze over the bay window on the right side of the facade. Within that frieze, you'll see several more "A's" sprouting from branches (*amatller* means "almond tree"). The reliefs above the smaller windows show off the hobbies of the Amatller clan: Find the cherubs holding the early box camera, the open book, and the amphora jug (which the family collected). Look through the second-floor bay window to see the corkscrew column. For info on tours of the interior, ✿ see page 120.

For another dimension of Modernisme, peek into the ground-floor windows of the Bagues Joieria jewelry shop and notice the slinky pieces by Spanish Art Nouveau jeweler Masriera.

▶ Now head left, to the end of the block. There, on the corner, you'll find...

Casa Lleó Morera (#35)

This paella-like mix of styles is the work of architect Lluís Domènech i Montaner, who also designed the Palace of Catalan Music. The lower floors have classical columns and a Greek-temple-like bay window. (Notice the real marble column—supporting nothing but some aristocrat's ego—placed for all to see behind the bay window.) Farther up are Gothic balconies of rosettes and tracery, while the upper part has faux Moorish stucco work. The whole thing is ornamented with fantastic griffins, angels, and fish. Flanking the third-story windows are figures holding the exciting inventions of the day—the camera, light bulb, and gramophone—designed to demonstrate just how modern the homeowners were in this age of Modernisme. The wonderful interior is open to the public for limited guided tours (✪ see page 121).

▶ *From here, it's four long blocks to Gaudí's Modernista masterpiece, La Pedrera. While the easiest route is to simply turn around and plow back up Passeig de Gràcia—passing top-end shops—it's more interesting to detour around the block. From this corner, walk up Carrer del Consell de Cent, past galleries, high-end shops, and a Starbucks, to another splashy Eixample boulevard—Rambla de Catalunya. When you hit this delightful street, go into the park-like median strip and turn right.*

❾ Rambla de Catalunya

As you head up Rambla de Catalunya, you'll find a narrower, more manageable street lined by inviting cafés and shops—boutiques that are still upscale, but generally more local and unique than those on the main drag.

After one block, a half-block detour (to the right) on Carrer d'Aragó gets you to the **Fundació Antoni Tàpies,** dedicated to the 20th-century abstract artist from Barcelona. The Montaner-designed building sums up the Modernist credo: modern brick, iron, and glass materials; playful decorative motifs; and a spacious, functional, and light-filled interior.

Hometown boy Tàpies' modern art museum

Casa Milà—Gaudí's icon of Modernisme

The tangled rooftop is called "The Cloud and the Chair." It's pricey to enter (€7), but fans will enjoy Tàpies' distinct mud-caked canvases. Tàpies (1923-2012) laid the canvas on the floor, covered it with wet varnish, and sprinkled in dust, dirt, and paint. Then he drew simple designs in the still-wet goop, capturing the primitive power of cavemen tracing the first art in mud with a stick.

▶ *Continue up the median of Rambla de Catalunya. When you get to Carrer de Provença, turn right and make your way to...*

❿ La Pedrera (Casa Milà)

This Gaudí exterior laughs down on the crowds filling Passeig de Gràcia. La Pedrera ("The Quarry") has a much-photographed roller coaster of melting-ice-cream eaves. This is Barcelona's quintessential Modernista building and was Gaudí's last major work (1906-1910) before he dedicated his final years to the Sagrada Família.

The building has a steel structural skeleton to support its weight (a new construction technique at the time). Gaudí's planned statues of the Virgin Mary and archangels were vetoed by the owner. If you have time—and the line's not too long—consider touring the house's interior and rooftop (✪ see page 122). Or just take a peek inside the main atrium for free.

▶ *Our walk is over. From here, you can head back to Plaça de Catalunya—it's a straight shot, seven blocks down Passeig de Gràcia. The Diagonal Metro station near La Pedrera, on the L3 (green) line, has easy connections to Plaça de Catalunya and other key stops.*

But for those with a little more energy, consider exploring some sights...

Nearby

A few steps up Passeig de Gràcia from La Pedrera, the fun **Vinçon** shop has stylish office and home furnishings. Two blocks farther up you run into **Avinguda Diagonal,** the aptly named boulevard that slashes diagonally through the Eixample grid. Two buildings along Diagonal were designed by Josep Puig i Cadafalch: the plateresque **Palau Baró de Quadras** (Diagonal 373), which is now a cultural center that's free to enter, and the distinctively turreted **Casa de les Punxes** ("House of Spikes," at #416).

If you continue north across Diagonal, you enter **Gràcia,** a neighborhood with a small town feel, narrower streets, and a youthful student scene. There you'll find **Hotel Casa Fuster** (Passeig de Gràcia 132), a fine

Modernista building by Lluís Domènech i Montaner that hosts jazz at night (✪ see page 175) and was featured in Woody Allen's film *Vicky Cristina Barcelona*.

A great place to end your explorations is back at the intersection of Passeig de Gràcia and Diagonal, where you'll find the Catalunya TI (at Passeig de Gràcia 107). Enter through the gate to the left of the TI entrance to discover an enjoyable little **park**—a tropical oasis in the heart of the city.

▶ *From the intersection of Passeig de Gràcia and Diagonal, you have several transportation options:*

*The handy **L3 (green) Metro** leaves from the Diagonal Metro stop, going to Plaça de Catalunya, Liceu (middle of the Ramblas), and Drassanes (bottom of the Ramblas).*

*The **L5 (blue) Metro** (enter the Diagonal Metro one block west on Carrer del Rosselló) goes to Sagrada Família.*

***Bus #24** goes to Gaudí's Park Güell. Catch it on Passeig de Gràcia just south of Diagonal, same side of street as La Pedrera; get off at the Carretera Carmel-Parc Güell stop.*

Sagrada Família Tour

Architect Antoni Gaudí's most famous and awe-inspiring work is this un-finished, super-sized church. With its cake-in-the-rain facade and other-worldly spires, the church is an icon of Barcelona and its trademark Modernista style. As an architect, Gaudí's foundations were classics, na-ture, and religion. The church represents all three.

Nearly a century after his death, people continue to toil to bring Gaudí's designs to life. There's something powerful about a community of committed people with a vision, working on a church that won't be finished in their lifetime—as was standard in the Gothic age. It's a testament to the generations of architects, sculptors, stonecutters, and donors who've been caught up in the audacity of Gaudí's astonishing vision. If there's any building on earth I'd like to see, it's the Sagrada Família...finished.

ORIENTATION

Cost: Church–€15, €18.50 combo-ticket covers church (no towers) and Gaudí House Museum at Park Güell (✪ see page 123).

Hours: Daily April-Sept 9:00-20:00, Oct-March 9:00-18:00.

Advance Tickets: To avoid lines, you can buy tickets online in advance for a specific entry time to the church and towers. Book at www.sagrada familia.cat and print tickets at home.

Crowd-Beating Tips: To minimize waiting, arrive right at 9:00 (when the church opens) or after 16:00. To skip the line, buy advance tickets, take a tour, or hire a private guide.

Getting There: The Sagrada Família Metro stop puts you right on the doorstep: Exit toward Plaça de la Sagrada Família. The church address is Carrer de Mallorca 401.

Information: Tel. 932-073-031, www.sagradafamilia.cat.

Getting In: The ticket windows are on the west side of the church, at the Passion Facade. If you already have tickets, head straight for the Nativity Facade (in front of Plaça de Gaudí), where you'll find entry lines for individuals. Show your ticket to the guard, who will direct you to the right line.

Tours: English-language tours (€4.50, 50 minutes) run daily at 11:00, 12:00, 13:00, and 15:00; no noon tours Mon-Fri in Nov-April (choose tour time when you buy ticket). Or rent the good 1.5-hour audioguide (€4.50).

Tower Elevators: Two different elevators (€4.50 each, best to reserve online to get your tower ticket time in sync with your church visit; otherwise buy tickets at main church ticket office) take you partway up the towers for a great view of the city and the church. The easier option is the Passion Facade elevator (no walking required). The Nativity Facade elevator lets you cross the dizzying bridge between the towers, but you'll need to take the stairs all the way down.

Length of This Tour: Allow 1.5 hours.

Background—A Dream Made Real

For more than 130 years, Barcelona has labored to bring Antoni Gaudí's vision to reality. In 1883, Gaudí signed up for the fledgling project, imagining a Gothic-style church with his own Art Nouveau/Modernisme touches. He labored on the Sagrada Família for 43 years. At his death (1926), the church was about 20 percent complete. Since then, construction has moved forward in fits and starts. Like Gothic churches of medieval times, the design has evolved over the decades.

The Spanish Civil War (1936-39) halted all work. In the 1950s, building resumed, though slowly. The pace picked up considerably with the advent of computer technology (1980s) and the energy of the '92 Olympics. In 2010, the main nave was finished enough to host a consecration mass by the pope (as a Catholic church, Sagrada Família is used for services, though irregularly).

Today it's still a work in progress, with a long way to go. The site bristles with cranking cranes, rusty forests of rebar, and scaffolding. The present architect has been at it since 1985. The work is funded exclusively by private donations and entry fees. There is visible progress, year after year. As I stepped inside on my last visit, the brilliance of Gaudí's vision for the interior was apparent.

The church should be finished by 2026, for the 100th anniversary of Gaudí's death. Make a date to attend the dedication with your kids or grandkids...to teach them a lesson in delayed gratification.

THE TOUR BEGINS

▶ *Start outside the Nativity Facade (where the entry lines for individuals are located), on the eastern side of the church. Before heading to the entrance, take in the...*

❶ View of the Exterior

Stand and imagine how grand this church will be when completed. The four 330-foot spires topped with crosses are just a fraction of this mega-church. When finished, the church will have 18 spires. Four will stand at each of the three entrances. Rising above those will be four taller towers, dedicated to the four Evangelists. A tower dedicated to Mary will rise still higher—400 feet. And in the very center of the complex will stand the grand 560-foot Jesus tower, topped with a cross that will shine like a spiritual lighthouse, visible even from out at sea.

The Nativity Facade, where tourists enter today, is only a side entrance to the church. The grand main entrance will be around to the left. That means that the nine-story apartment building will eventually have to be torn down to accommodate it. The three facades—Nativity, Passion,

Nativity Facade—Gaudí completed this side, but much (including the grand main entrance beneath the Glory Facade) is unfinished.

Sagrada Família

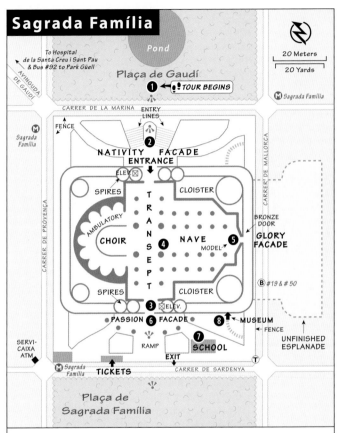

To Hospital de la Santa Creu i Sant Pau & Bus #92 to Park Güell

AVINGUDA DE GAUDÍ

Pond

Plaça de Gaudí

1 ← ☝ **TOUR BEGINS**

Ⓜ Sagrada Família

20 Meters

20 Yards

CARRER DE LA MARINA

ENTRY LINES

FENCE

Ⓜ Sagrada Família

2

NATIVITY FACADE
ENTRANCE

ELEV ⊠

SPIRES

CLOISTER

CARRER DE MALLORCA

CARRER DE PROVENÇA

AMBULATORY

CHOIR

T R A N S E P T

NAVE

MODEL

4

5

BRONZE DOOR

GLORY FACADE

Ⓑ #19 & #50

SPIRES

CLOISTER

⊠ ELEV.

3

PASSION **6** **FACADE**

8 ↑

MUSEUM

← FENCE

UNFINISHED ESPLANADE

SERVI-CAIXA ATM ◆

RAMP

7

SCHOOL

EXIT

Ⓣ

Ⓜ Sagrada Família

TICKETS

CARRER DE SARDENYA

Plaça de Sagrada Família

---

1 View of the Exterior

2 Nativity Facade

3 Atrium

4 Interior & 4 Red Porphyry Columns

5 Glory Facade

6 Passion Facade

7 School

8 Ramp to Museum

and Glory—will chronicle Christ's life from birth to death to resurrection. Despite his boldly modern architectural vision, Gaudí was fundamentally traditional and deeply religious. He designed the Sagrada Família to be a bastion of solid Christian values in a fast-changing city.

Though Gaudí made the original design, he knew it could never be completed in his lifetime. (He enjoyed saying, "My client (God) is not in a hurry.") He gave his blessing to later architects to modify his designs and rely on their own muses for inspiration. But every new plan brings controversy. Stay true to Gaudí's Gothic-Modernista foundation, or use styles that reflect the world today? Discuss.

▶ *Now approach the...*

❷ Nativity Facade

This is the only part of the church essentially finished in Gaudí's lifetime. The four spires decorated with his unmistakably nonlinear sculpture mark this facade as part of his original design. Mixing Gothic-style symbolism, images from nature, and Modernista asymmetry, the Nativity Facade is the best example of Gaudí's original vision, and it established the template for future architects who would work on the building.

The facade, which faces the rising sun, is full of symbolism; its theme is Christ's birth. A statue above the doorway shows Mary, Joseph, and Baby Jesus in the manger. It's the Holy Family—or "Sagrada Família"—to whom this church is dedicated. A stylized Alpha-and-Omega is over the door (which faces the setting sun). Jesus, hanging on the cross, has hair made of an open book, symbolizing the word of God.

To the left of the door is a grid of numbers, always adding up to 33—Jesus' age at the time of his death. The distinct face of the man below and left of Christ is a memorial to Gaudí. Flanking the doorway are the three Magi and adoring shepherds. Other statues show Jesus as a young carpenter and angels playing musical instruments. Higher up on the facade, in the arched niche, Jesus crowns Mary triumphantly.

The four **spires** are dedicated to apostles, and they repeatedly bear the word "Sanctus," or holy. Their colorful ceramic caps symbolize the miters (formal hats) of bishops. The shorter spires (to the left) symbolize the Eucharist (communion), alternating between a chalice with grapes and a communion host with wheat.

Now look high above: The two-ton figure suspended between the towers is the soul of Jesus, ascending to heaven.

Nativity Facade with Holy Family, the Sagrada Família to whom the church is dedicated

▶ *Enter the church. As you pass through the* ❸ **atrium,** *look down at the fine porphyry floor (with scenes of Jesus' entry into Jerusalem), and look right to see one of the* **elevators** *up to the towers. For now, continue into the...*

❹ Interior

Typical of even the most traditional Spanish churches, the floor plan is in the shape of a Latin cross, 300 feet long and 200 feet wide. Ultimately, the church will encompass 48,000 square feet, accommodating 8,000 worshippers. The nave's roof is 150 feet high. The crisscross arches of the ceiling (the vaults) show off Gaudí's distinctive engineering. The church's roof and flooring were completed in 2010—just in time for Pope Benedict XVI to arrive and consecrate the church.

Part of Gaudí's religious vision was a love for nature. He said, "Nothing is invented; it's written in nature." Like the trunks of trees, these **columns** (56 in all) blossom with life, complete with branches, leaves, and knot-like capitals. The columns are a variety of colors—brown clay, gray granite, dark-gray basalt. The taller columns are 72 feet tall; the shorter ones are exactly half that.

The angled columns form many **arches.** You'll see both parabolas (U-shaped) and hyperbolas (flatter, elliptical shapes). Gaudí's starting point was the Gothic pointed arch used in medieval churches. But he tweaked it after meticulous study of which arches are best at bearing weight.

Little **windows** let light filter in like the canopy of a rainforest, giving both privacy and an intimate connection with God. The clear glass will gradually be replaced by stained glass to match Gaudí's vision of a symphony of colored light.

High up at the back half of the church, the U-shaped **choir**—suspended above the nave—can seat 1,000. The singers will eventually be backed by four organs (there's one now).

Work your way up the grand nave, walking through this forest of massive columns. At the center of the church stand four **red porphyry columns,** each marked with an Evangelist's symbol and name in Catalan: angel (Mateu), lion (Marc), bull (Luc), and eagle (Joan). These columns support a ceiling vault that's 200 feet high—and eventually will also support the central steeple, the 560-foot Jesus tower with the shining cross. The steeple will be further supported by four underground pylons, each

The vast nave soars up 150 feet, lined with columns inspired by both Gothic forms and trees.

Glory Facade's bronze door

Passion Facade's stark, semi-abstract sculpture

consisting of 8,000 tons of cement. It will be the tallest church steeple in the world.

Stroll behind the altar through the **ambulatory** to reach a small chapel set aside for prayer and meditation. Look through windows down at the **crypt** (which holds the tomb of Gaudí).

▶ *Head to the far end of the church, to what will eventually be the main entrance. Just inside the door, find the **bronze model** of the floor plan for the completed church. Facing the doors, look high up to see Subirachs' statue of one of Barcelona's patron saints, **George (Jordi).** While you can't see it, imagine what outside these doors will someday be the...*

❺ Glory Facade

Study the life-size image of the **bronze door,** emblazoned with the Lord's Prayer in Catalan, surrounded by "Give us this day our daily bread" in 50 languages. If you were able to walk through the actual door, you'd be face-to-face with...drab, doomed apartment blocks. In the 1950s, the mayor of Barcelona, figuring this day would never really come, sold the land destined for the church project. Now the city must buy back these buildings in order to complete Gaudí's vision: that of a grand esplanade leading to this main entry. Four towers will rise. The facade's sculpture will represent how the soul passes through death, faces the Last Judgment, avoids the pitfalls of hell, and finds its way to eternal glory with God. Gaudí purposely left the facade's design open for later architects—stay tuned.

▶ *Head back up the nave, and exit through the left transept. Notice the second **elevator** up to the towers. Once outside, back up as far as you can to take in the...*

❻ Passion Facade

Judge for yourself how well Gaudí's original vision has been carried out by later artists. The Passion Facade's four spires were designed by Gaudí and completed (quite faithfully) in 1976. But the lower part was only inspired by Gaudí's designs. The stark sculptures were interpreted freely (and controversially) by Josep Maria Subirachs (1927-2014), who completed the work in 2005.

Subirachs tells the story of Christ's torture and execution. The various scenes—Last Supper, betrayal, whipping, and so on—zigzag up from bottom to top, culminating in Christ's crucifixion over the doorway. The style is severe and unadorned, quite different from Gaudí's signature playfulness. But the bone-like archways are closely based on Gaudí's original designs. And Gaudí had made it clear that this facade should be grim and terrifying.

▶ *Now head into the small building outside the Passion Façade. This is the...*

❼ School

Gaudí erected this school for the children of the workers building the church. Today it includes exhibits about the design and engineering of the church, along with a classroom and a replica of Gaudí's desk as it was the day he died.

▶ *Back outside, head down the ramp, where you'll find WCs and the entrance to the...*

❽ Museum

Housed in what will someday be the church's crypt, the museum displays Gaudí's original **models and drawings,** and chronicles the progress of

The Nativity Facade celebrates all life.

Gaudí completed this part in his lifetime.

construction over the last 130-plus years. Upon entering, you'll see **photos** (including one of the master himself) and a **timeline** illustrating how construction work has progressed from Gaudí's day to now. Before turning into the main hall, find **three different visions** for this church.

As you wander, notice how the **plaster models,** used for the church's construction, don't always match the finished product—these are ideas, not blueprints set in stone. The Passion Facade model shows Gaudí's original vision, with which Subirachs tinkered very freely. The models also

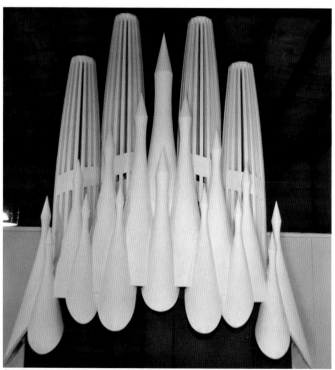

Gaudí's models in the museum give future architects plenty of ideas to chew on.

make clear the influence of nature. The columns seem light, with branches springing forth and capitals that look like palm trees.

Turn up the main hallway, walking under a huge **model of the nave,** and past some original **sculptures** from the different facades (on the left). Farther along, a small hallway on the left leads to some original Gaudí architectural **sketches** in a dimly lit room and a worthwhile 20-minute **movie** (continuously shown in Catalan with English subtitles).

From the end of this hall, you have another opportunity to look down into the crypt and at **Gaudí's tomb.** Gaudí lived on the site for more than a decade and is buried in the Neo-Gothic 19th-century crypt (also viewable from the apse). There's a move afoot to make Gaudí a saint. Perhaps someday his tomb will be a place of pilgrimage.

On the right, you can peek into a busy **workshop** still used for making the same kind of plaster models Gaudí used to envision the final product in three dimensions.

▶ *Our tour is over. To return to central Barcelona, hop on the Metro, or catch a bus on Carrer de Mallorca (by the Glory Facade). Bus #19 stops near the Barcelona Cathedral. Bus #50 goes to the heart of the Eixample (corner of Gran Via de les Corts Catalanes and Passeig de Gràcia).*

Park Güell (✪ see page 123) is two (uphill) miles to the northwest of Sagrada Família. A taxi there costs around €10-12. Or you could take the Metro to the Joanic stop, then catch bus #116.

Sights

Barcelona's array of sights is surprisingly varied. There are great walking neighborhoods—the Ramblas, Barri Gòtic, and El Born—for shopping, nightlife, and people-watching. There's the city's Modernista legacy, including Gaudí's Sagrada Família, La Pedrera, and Park Güell. You can also choose from medieval churches and colorful markets, spontaneous outbreaks of folk dancing and quirky museums, Roman ruins and the modern art of Picasso and Miró.

I list sights by neighborhood for handy sightseeing. When you see a ✪ in a listing, it means the sight is covered in much more depth in one of my walks or self-guided tours.

✪ For tips on sightseeing and avoiding lines by making advance reservations, see page 170. Also, be sure to check www.ricksteves.com/update for any significant changes that may have occurred since this book was printed.

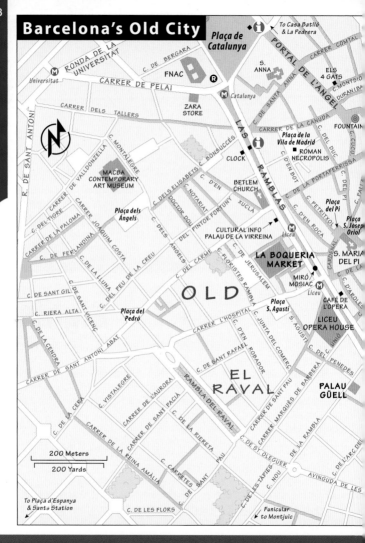

Barcelona's Old City

Plaça de Catalunya

To Casa Batlló & La Pedrera

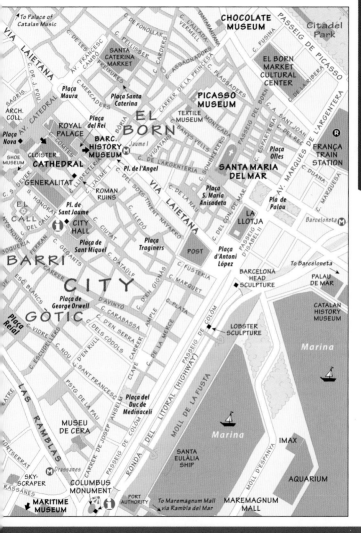

To Palace of Catalan Music

VIA LAIETANA

C. DE LES
C. DE J. POU
AV. DE J. POU
SAGRIS.
ARCH. COLL.

Plaça Nova

SHOE MUSEUM

CLOISTER

CATHEDRAL

GENERALITAT

EL CALL

BARRI

CITY

GÒTIC

Plaça Reial

LAS RAMBLAS

C. DE FONOLLAR
C. DE LES FELISSERS
C. D'ASSAONADORS
TANTARANTANA
C. L'ALLADA VERMELL
CHOCOLATE MUSEUM

PASSEIG DE PICASSO

Citadel Park

SANTA CATERINA MARKET

AV. FRANCESC CAMBÓ
C. MERCADERS
C. FLASSADERS
C. DE LA PRINCESA

Plaça Maura

Plaça Santa Caterina

EL BORN

ROYAL PALACE

BARC. HISTORY MUSEUM

Plaça del Rei

TEXTILE MUSEUM

PICASSO MUSEUM

EL BORN MARKET CULTURAL CENTER

C. FUSINA

C. DE LA RIBERA

PASSEIG DEL BORN

A. SANT JOAN

PASSEIG DEL REI

A. DEL REI

C. ESPARTERIA

Plaça Olles

SANTA MARIA DEL MAR

FRANÇA TRAIN STATION

C. DUANA

Barceloneta

Barceloneta

PALAU DE MAR

CATALAN HISTORY MUSEUM

Marina

Jaume I

C. DE L'ARGENTERIA

ROMAN RUINS

Pl. de l'Angel

VIA LAIETANA

Plaça S. Maria Anisadeta

Plaça S. Maria Anisadeta

Pla de Palau

LA LLOTJA

Plaça d'Antoni López

POST

BARCELONA HEAD SCULPTURE

To Barceloneta

Pl. de Sant Jaume

CITY HALL

Plaça de Sant Miquel

Plaça Traginers

Plaça de George Orwell

D'AVINYÓ
C. CARABASSA
C. D'EN SERRA
C. DELS CODOLS
C. D'EN RULL
C. SANT FRANCESC
PSTG DE LA PAU

LOBSTER SCULPTURE

Marina

SANTA EULÀLIA SHIP

IMAX

AQUARIUM

MUSEU DE CERA

Plaça del Duc de Medinaceli

MARITIME MUSEUM

SKY-SCRAPER

COLUMBUS MONUMENT

PORT AUTHORITY

To Maremagnum Mall via Rambla del Mar

MAREMAGNUM MALL

Drassanes

PASSEIG DE COLOM

RONDA DEL LITORAL (HIGHWAY)

MOLL DE LA FUSTA

MOLL D'ESPANYA

On or Near the Ramblas

▲▲▲The Ramblas

From Plaça de Catalunya to the harborfront, this colorful, pedestrian-friendly boulevard leads through the heart of the Old City. It's a people-watcher's dream.

✪ For a self-guided tour, see the Ramblas Ramble chapter.

▲La Boqueria Market

Discover a wide array of vendors selling Catalan edibles inside this covered hall. It's crowded and touristy but ultra-atmospheric.

✪ See page 24 in the Ramblas Ramble chapter.

▲Palau Güell

This early mansion by Antoni Gaudí shows the architect's first tentative steps toward his trademark curvy style. Even from the outside, you get a sense of this innovative apartment, the first of Gaudí's Modernista buildings. As this is early Gaudí (built 1886-1890), it's darker and more Neo-Gothic than his more famous later projects. The two parabolic-arch doorways and elaborate wrought-iron work signal his emerging nonlinear style.

Inside, you tour intricately decorated living spaces (dining room, bedrooms, and domed central hall) and learn about Gaudí and the Güell family. The highlight is the rooftop, where Gaudí slathered the chimneys with bits of colored glass, tile, and marble to create a forest of giant upside-down ice-cream cones. I'd skip Palau Güell if you plan to visit the more interesting La Pedrera (✪ see page 122).

▶ *€12, free first Sun of the month. Open Tue-Sun 10:00-20:00, Nov-March until 17:30, closed Mon, last entry one hour before closing. Buy timed-entry tickets in advance, either on-site or online. Ticket includes engaging audioguide. Located a half-block off the Ramblas at Carrer Nou de la Rambla 3, Metro: Liceu or Drassanes. Tel. 934-725-775, www.palauguell.cat.*

▲Plaça Reial

This genteel-feeling square is lined with palm trees and touristy (but still atmospheric) bars and restaurants.

Palau Güell's rooftop chimneys by Gaudí

Maritime Museum, the city's salty legacy

⚙ See page 29 in the Ramblas Ramble chapter, and check out recommendations for eateries (⚙ page 150) and nightlife (⚙ page 174).

▲Maritime Museum (Museu Marítim)

This excellent museum is housed in a well-preserved 14th-century shipyard. The permanent collection is closed for renovation, but the temporary exhibits are worthwhile. The cavernous halls evoke the days when Catalunya's merchant fleet ruled the Mediterranean, and its factories could crank out a galley a week. When the permanent collection reopens, it'll cover the salty history from the 13th to the 20th century. A huge and richly decorated replica of a royal galley remains on display, and your ticket includes entry to the *Santa Eulàlia* schooner docked just a short walk from the Columbus Monument.

▶ *Museum—€7, free on Sun from 15:00, open daily 10:00-20:00, nice café in courtyard, Avinguda de la Drassanes, Metro: Drassanes. Santa Eulàlia—€3 without museum visit, open Tue-Sun 10:00-20:30, except Sat when it opens at 14:00, Nov-March until 17:30, closed Mon. Tel. 933-429-920, www.mmb.cat.*

Columbus Monument (Monument a Colóm)

This 200-foot-tall monument commemorates Columbus' stop in Barcelona following his first trip to America. A tight four-person elevator takes you to a glassed-in observation area at the top for congested but sweeping views, and there's a small TI inside the monument's base.

⚙ See page 30 of the Ramblas Ramble chapter.

Golondrinas Cruises

Boats called *golondrinas* take tourists for sightseeing spins around the harbor. As Barcelona's skyline isn't all that striking from the water (and there's no guide), these trips are worthwhile mainly if you just like boat rides.

▶ *Harbor tours—€7.20 for 40 minutes, €15 for 90 minutes. Boats run daily 11:30-19:00, more in summer, fewer in winter. Located at the harbor, near the Columbus Monument, Metro: Drassanes;* ✪ *for location see the map on page 4. Tel. 934-423-106, www.lasgolondrinas.com.*

The Barri Gòtic

Stretching from Plaça de Catalunya to the harbor, the area east of the Ramblas is the old medieval quarter. The closest Metro stop is Jaume I.

For more details on this area and several of the following sights, see the ✪ Barri Gòtic Walk chapter.

▲Cathedral of Barcelona

The city's 14th-century, Gothic-style cathedral (with a Neo-Gothic facade) has played a significant role in Barcelona's history—but as far as grand cathedrals go, this one is relatively unexciting. Still, it's worth a visit to see its richly decorated chapels, finely carved choir, tomb of St. Eulàlia, and restful cloister with gurgling fountains and resident geese.

✪ See the Cathedral of Barcelona Tour chapter.

▲ *Sardana* Dances

If you're in town on a weekend, you can see the *sardana,* a patriotic dance in which Barcelonans—young and old—link hands and dance in a circle. For some it's a highly symbolic, politically charged action representing Catalan unity—but for most it's just a fun chance to kick up their heels. Participants put their belongings in the center, join hands, and hop and sway to the music, *Zorba the Greek*-style, while the band plays odd-looking oboes, brass instruments, and bongos. All are welcome, even tourists with two left feet.

▶ *The free dances, which last an hour or two, are held in the square in front of the cathedral on Sundays at 12:00 and occasionally on Saturdays at 18:00 (none in Aug; Metro: Jaume I).*

Frederic Marès Museum (Museu Frederic Marès)

This eclectic collection assembled by local sculptor and packrat Frederic

Locals and tourists dance the *sardana*.

Frederic Marès Museum—more than statues

Marès (1893-1991) sprawls around a peaceful courtyard. There's lots of sculpture, from ancient to Gothic to the early 20th century. More interesting is Marès' "Collector's Cabinet" of everyday 19th-century bric-a-brac: rooms upon rooms of scissors, fans, nutcrackers, stamps, pipes, snuff boxes, pocket watches, bicycles, and dolls. And in Marès' study are several sculptures by the artist himself. The tranquil courtyard café (summer only, until 22:00) offers a pleasant break, even when the museum is closed.

▶ *€4.20, free all day first Sun of month and other Sun from 15:00. Open Tue-Sat 10:00-19:00, Sun 11:00-20:00, closed Mon. Audioguide-€1. Located to the left of the cathedral at Plaça de Sant Iu 5, Metro: Jaume I. Tel. 932-563-500, www.museumares.bcn.cat.*

Shoe Museum (Museu del Calçat)

Shoe lovers enjoy this tiny museum of footwear in glass display cases, watched over by an earnest attendant (no English descriptions). You'll see shoes from the 1700s to today: fancy ladies' boots, Tibetan moccasins, big clown shoes, boots that have been to Mt. Everest, and shoes of minor celebrities. The huge shoes at the entry are designed to fit the feet of the statue atop the Columbus Monument at the bottom of the Ramblas.

▶ *€2.50. Open Tue-Sun 11:00-14:00, closed Mon. Plaça Sant Felip Neri 5, Metro: Jaume I. Tel. 933-014-533.*

Roman Temple of Augustus (Temple Roma d'August)

Tucked inside a small medieval courtyard, four columns from an ancient temple of Augustus are a reminder of Barcelona's Roman origins.

✪ See page 50 of the Barri Gòtic Walk chapter.

▲Barcelona History Museum
(Museu d'Història de Barcelona: Plaça del Rei)

Barcelona has thrived for 2,500 years. It's been a Roman retirement colony, a maritime power, a dynamo of the Industrial Age, and a cradle for all things modern. This museum—housed in medieval buildings that rise over excavated Roman ruins—lets you walk through that history. Posted information is in Catalan, Spanish, and English, and you'll also find abundant English handouts. The included English audioguide provides informative, if dry, descriptions.

Start with the 10-minute introductory video on the first floor; it plays alternately in Catalan, Spanish, and English. Then take an elevator down 65 feet (and 2,000 years) to stroll the ruins of Roman Barcino. The history is so strong here, you can smell it. The route leads you through areas used for laundering and dyeing garments, the remains of a fish-processing factory, winemaking facilities, bits of an early Christian church, and an exhibit in the 11th-century count's palace that shows you Barcelona's glory days in the Middle Ages.

Finally, head upstairs to see a model of the city from the early 16th century. From here, you can also enter Tinell Hall (part of the former Royal Palace), with its long, graceful, rounded vaults. Nearby, step into the 14th-century Chapel of St. Agatha if it's hosting a free temporary exhibit.

▶ *€7, free all day first Sun of month and other Sun from 15:00. Open Tue-Sat 10:00-19:00, Sun 10:00-20:00, closed Mon. Includes audioguide except during free times. Located on Plaça del Rei, enter on Carrer del Veguer, Metro: Jaume I. Tel. 932-562-122.*

El Born and Nearby

The neighborhood called El Born (also known as La Ribera) is a bohemian-chic paradise of funky shops, upscale eateries, a colorful market hall, unique boutiques, the Picasso Museum, and rollicking nightlife. It feels wonderfully local, with a higher ratio of Barcelonans to tourists than most other city-center zones. The heart of the neighborhood is the narrow lanes sprouting around Passeig del Born and the Church of Santa Maria del Mar (Metro: Jaume I).

▲El Born Walk

Stroll through this rough-but-gentrifying neighborhood from the Cathedral

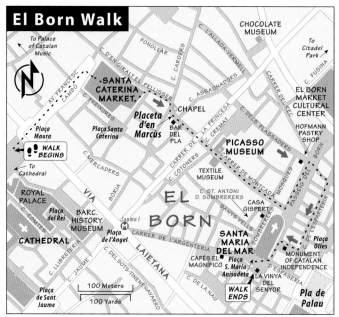

El Born Walk

To Palace
of Catalan
Music

CHOCOLATE
MUSEUM

C. L'ALLADA-VERMELL

To
Citadel
Park

FONOLLAR

C. CARDERS

C. FUSINA

CARRER DEL REC

AV. FRANCESC CAMBÓ

C. D'EN GIRALT EL PELLISSER

C. FREIXURES

SANTA
CATERINA
MARKET.

C. ASSAONADORS

EL BORN
MARKET
CULTURAL
CENTER

Placeta
d'en
Marcús

CHAPEL

BAR
DEL
PLA

C. DELS FLASSADERS

HOFMANN
PASTRY
SHOP

Plaça
Maura

Plaça Santa
Caterina

C. DE LA PRINCESA

C. CREMAT

PICASSO
MUSEUM

PASSEIG DEL BORN

WALK
BEGINS

C. MERCADERS

C. COTONERS

CARRER DE MONTCADA

To
Cathedral

TEXTILE
MUSEUM

C. ST. ANTONI
D. SOMBRERERS

ROYAL
PALACE

VIA

BÒRIA

EL

CASA
GISPERT

C. MOSQUES

LA PARTERIA

Plaça
del Rei

BARC.
HISTORY
MUSEUM

BORN

BANYS VELLS

C. COMES

Jaume I

Plaça
de l'Angel

SANTA
MARIA
DEL MAR

SOMBRERERS

Plaça
Olles

CATHEDRAL

C. LLIBRETERIA

CARRER DE L'ARGENTERIA

CAFÉS EL
MAGNÍFICO

Plaça
S. Maria

MONUMENT
OF CATALAN
INDEPENDENCE

C. DEL SOTS-TINENT NAVARRO

LAIETANA

Plaça
S. Maria
Anisadeta

LA VINYA
DEL
SENYOR

C. DE LA NAU

WALK
ENDS

Pla de
Palau

Plaça
de Sant
Jaume

100 Meters

100 Yards

of Barcelona to the Church of Santa Maria del Mar. I'll only give directions, not lengthy descriptions, and let El Born's authenticity speak for itself.

Facing the **cathedral,** turn left. As you cross Plaça d'Antoni Maura and traffic-choked Via Laietana, you enter El Born. Continue toward the undulating roof of **Santa Caterina Market.** It's the local choice for buying jamón, cheese, and colorful produce, and a good place to enjoy inviting eateries (for more on the market, see the listing later in this section).

Pass through the market and exit out its back end, angle left, then turn right on tiny Carrer d'en Giralt el Pellisser. Continue past the humble 12th-century church (supposedly Barcelona's oldest) until the street becomes **Carrer de Montcada**—lined with art galleries, shops, and eateries.

You'll pop out onto **Passeig del Born,** the long boulevard that's the neighborhood center and a popular springboard for exploring tapas bars, fun restaurants, and nightspots in the narrow streets all around. At the far end to your left is a steel-frame, 19th-century market hall housing the

El Born Cultural Center, home to a permanent Barcelona 1700 exhibit, temporary displays, medieval excavations, and a café (free to enter, €6 for exhibits).

Back on Passeig del Born, turn left on the arcaded Carrer del Rec shopping street. Then turn right along **Carrer de l'Esparteria.** Explore this area and its side streets, rich with fashion boutiques, local craftsmen, and laundry drying from wrought-iron balconies—classic Barcelona.

Turn right down Carrer del Malcuinat, to the **Monument of Catalan Independence.** This marks the site of a mass grave. On September 11, 1714, Bourbon King Philip V conquered independent Barcelona, massacred the resisters, and established two centuries of dominance by the Madrid government. Catalan language and culture were outlawed. Today Catalunya is thriving, but the monument's flame burns eternally for the "Catalan Alamo," and 9/11 remains a sobering anniversary. (When Catalans head to the toilet, they still say, "I'm going to Philip's house.")

The 14th-century **Church of Santa Maria del Mar** anchors El Born. The unadorned interior—naked in all its pure Catalan-Gothic glory—features tree-like columns that inspired Gaudí's Sagrada Família, colorful chapels, and modern stained-glass windows. For more on the church, see the listing later in this section.

Near the church, you can sip a drink at La Vinya del Senyor wine bar (facing the church entrance), buy a bottle at Vila Vinateca wine shop (Carrer des Agullers 7), sample the city's "best" coffee at Cafés El Magnífico (Carrer de l'Argenteria 64), and inhale roasting nuts at Casa Gispert (Carrer dels Sombrerers 23). You're at the heart of Barcelona's most colorful bohemian quarter.

Palace of Catalan Music, a Modernista gem

Santa Caterina Market in El Born

▲▲▲Picasso Museum (Museu Picasso)

Pablo Picasso may have made his career in Paris, but the years he spent in Barcelona—from ages 14 through 23—were among the most formative of his life. The museum focuses on those early years, while including a few representative works spanning his long life. It's undoubtedly the top collection of Picassos in his native country.

⚙ See the Picasso Museum Tour chapter.

▲▲Palace of Catalan Music (Palau de la Música Catalana)

This concert hall, built in just three years and finished in 1908, features an unexceptional exterior but boasts my favorite Modernista interior in town (by Lluís Domènech i Montaner). Its inviting arches lead you into the 2,138-seat hall, accessible only with a tour (or by attending a concert). A kaleidoscopic skylight features a choir singing around the sun, while playful carvings and mosaics celebrate music and Catalan culture. If you're interested in Modernisme, taking this tour is one of the best experiences in town—and helps balance the hard-to-avoid focus on Gaudí as "Mr. Modernisme."

▸ €18. 50-minute tours in English run daily every hour 10:00-15:00, tour times may change based on performance schedule, reserve tour tickets in person at the hall (open daily 9:30-15:30), by phone with a credit card (tel. 902-475-485), or online at www.palaumusica.cat (€1 fee). Located about six blocks northeast of the cathedral at Carrer Palau de la Música 4, Metro: Urquinaona.

Concerts: Music lovers see the hall's interior while attending a concert (300 per year, €20-50 tickets, see website for details, box office tel. 902-442-882).

▲Santa Caterina Market

This eye-catching market hall's colorful, rippling roof (2006) covers a delightful shopping zone that caters more to locals than to tourists. Come for the outlandish architecture, but stay for a chance to shop for a picnic without the tourist logjam of La Boqueria on the Ramblas. In addition to fresh produce, it has many inviting eateries.

▸ Open Mon-Sat 7:30-15:30, Thu-Fri until 20:30, closed Sun. Avinguda de Francesc Cambó 16, Metro: Jaume I. Tel. 933-195-740, www.mercat santacaterina.net.

Sights

▲Church of Santa Maria del Mar

This 14th-century church is the proud centerpiece of El Born. The "Cathedral of the Sea" was built entirely with local funds by wealthy shippers and merchants.

On the big front doors, notice the figures of workers who donated their time and sweat to build the church. The stone for the church was quarried at Montjuïc and had to be carried across town on the backs of porters.

Step inside. The church features a purely Catalan Gothic interior. During the Spanish Civil War (1936-1939), Catalan patriots fighting Franco burned the ornate Baroque decoration (carbon still blackens the ceiling), leaving behind this unadorned Gothic. The colorful windows come with modern themes. The tree-like columns inspired Gaudí's work on Sagrada Família. Befitting a church "of the sea," sailors traditionally left models of ships at the altar to win Mary's protection—one remains today.

▶ *Free admission daily 9:00-13:00 & 17:00-20:30, also open 13:00-17:00 with €5 ticket. €8 guided rooftop tours in summer; English tours on the hour Mon-Fri 12:00-16:00, Sat-Sun 11:00-16:00 summer tours run until 19:00. Plaça Santa Maria 1, Metro: Jaume I. Tel. 933-102-390.*

Chocolate Museum (Museu de la Xocolata)

Fun for chocolate lovers, this museum—operated by the local confectioners' guild—tells the story of chocolate from Aztecs to Europeans via the port of Barcelona, where it was first unloaded and processed. But the history lesson is just an excuse to show off some remarkably ornate candy sculptures. These works of edible art—which change every year but often include such themes as Don Quixote or Gaudí's dragon from Park Güell—are displayed in store windows for Easter or Christmas.

▶ *€5. Open Mon-Sat 10:00-19:00, summer until 20:00, Sun 10:00-15:00. Located a few blocks from the Picasso Museum at Carrer del Comerç 36, Metro: Jaume I. Tel. 932-687-878, www.museuxocolata.cat.*

Citadel Park (Parc de la Ciutadella)

In 1888, the site of a much-hated military citadel (representing the Madrid government's oppression) was transformed into the fairgrounds of an international exposition. The stately Triumphal Arch at the top of the park, celebrating the removal of the citadel, was the main entrance. Today the Citadel is Barcelona's most central, greenest park, complete with a zoo and museums of geology and zoology. It's a haven (especially on weekends) for happy families escaping the concrete and population density of modern Barcelona. Enjoy the ornamental fountain that the young Antoni Gaudí helped design, and consider renting a rowboat on the lake in the center of the park. Check out the tropical Umbracle greenhouse and the Hivernacle winter garden, which has a pleasant café. The zoo features tigers, hippos, and zebras plus a SeaWorld-like dolphin show.

▶ *Park—free, open daily 10:00 until dusk. Zoo—€20 for adults, €12 for kids 3-12, open daily in summer 10:00-20:00, hours vary by season, tel. 902-457-545, www.zoobarcelona.cat. Metro: Arc de Triomf, Barceloneta, or Ciutadella-Vila Olímpica.*

▲Barcelona's Beaches

This man-made Riviera is great for sunbathing or an evening paseo before dinner. Barcelona's beaches are like a resort island—complete with lounge chairs, volleyball, showers, WCs, and inviting beach bars called *chiringuitos*. Bike paths make the beaches great for joy-riding (✪ see page 168 for bike-rental places).

▶ *Located east of the El Born neighborhood, the sand starts in Barceloneta and stretches north. Metro: Barceloneta leaves you blocks away. To get closer, take bus #59 from the Ramblas or bus #D20 from the Columbus Monument to Barceloneta Park. Bus #V15 runs from Plaça de Catalunya to Barceloneta (near the W Hotel).*

The Eixample

The grid-patterned neighborhood north of Plaça de Catalunya (Metro: Passeig de Gràcia) is dotted with buildings in the Modernista style and

Santa Maria del Mar—"Catalan Gothic"

Take a vacation from museums at the beach.

brims with upscale stores and eateries. The center of this neighborhood is the **Block of Discord,** where three colorful Modernista facades—at Casa Batlló, Casa Amatller, and Casa Lleó Morera—by three different architects create a delightful "discord" along a single city block. If you're tempted to snap photos from the middle of the street, be careful: Gaudí died after being struck by a streetcar.

From the Block of Discord, you're just four blocks from Gaudí's La Pedrera, and a quick subway ride from his Sagrada Família.

✪ For more about this area, see the Eixample Walk chapter.

▲Casa Batlló

While the highlight is the roof, the interior of this Gaudí house is also interesting—and even more over-the-top than La Pedrera's. The house features a funky mushroom-shaped fireplace nook on the main floor, a blue-and-white-ceramic-slathered atrium, and an attic (with more parabolic arches). There's barely a straight line in the house. You can also get a close-up look at the dragon-inspired rooftop. Because preservation of the place is privately funded, the entrance fee is steep.

▶ *€21.50. Open daily 9:00-21:00, may close early for special events. Buy your ticket online in advance to avoid lines (especially long in the morning). Ticket includes good (if long-winded) audioguide, €3 videoguide shows rooms as they may have been. Passeig de Gràcia 41, Metro: Passeig de Gràcia. Tel. 932-160-306, www.casabatllo.cat.*

Casa Amatller

The middle residence of the Block of Discord can be visited with a guided tour that allows you to see the modernist interior design, including many

Block of Discord—three frisky facades

Casa Milà's parabola-shaped attic

Modernista Sights

For some visitors, Modernista architecture is Barcelona's main draw. Showpieces of the movement—the Block of Discord and Gaudí's La Pedrera—can be seen in the Eixample neighborhood. Nearby are two lesser-known works by Lluís Domènech i Montaner: Fundació Antoni Tàpies (around the corner from the Block of Discord, at Carrer d'Aragó 255) and Hotel Casa Fuster (directly across Avinguda de Diagonal, at the far end of a small park at Passeig de Gràcia 132). Also in the Eixample are two buildings by Josep Puig i Cadafalch: Palau Baró de Quadras (a few blocks east from the top of Passeig de Gràcia at Diagonal #373) and Casa de les Punxes ("House of Spikes," at #416).

At the northern edge of the Eixample is Gaudí's greatest piece of work, the yet-to-be-finished Sagrada Família church (❁ see page 123). Farther north is Park Güell, where Gaudí put his colorful stamp on 30 acres of greenery (❁ see page 123).

Other Modernista highlights include Gaudí's Palau Güell, just off the Ramblas (❁ see page 110); Lluís Domènech i Montaner's Palace of Catalan Music in El Born (❁ see page 117); and Josep Puig i Cadafalch's CaixaForum, at the base of Montjuïc (❁ see page 128). For information on Modernista sights, visit the TI on Plaça de Catalunya, which has a special desk just for Modernisme maniacs.

original pieces. If you don't want to pay for a ticket, simply admire its Neo-Catalan Gothic facade, with tiles and *esgrafiado* decoration, and step inside the foyer (free during opening hours) to see the modernist stained-glass door and ceiling, and an elaborate staircase.

▸ *€15 guided tour, daily 11:00-18:00, English tours at 11:00 and 15:00, advance tickets available online, Passeig de Gràcia 41, tel. 934-617-460, www.amatller.org.*

▲Casa Lleó Morera

This house, designed by Lluís Domènech i Montaner and finished in 1906, has one of the finest Modernista interiors in town. Access is by guided tour only, which begins with the history of the Lleó Morera family and a look at the detailing on the building's exterior. Inside, you'll marvel at finely crafted mosaics, ceramic work, wooden ceilings and doors, stone sculptures, and stained glass.

▶ €15 for 70-minute English tour, €12 for express 45-minute tour (mixed English, Spanish, and Catalan) open Tue-Sun, closed Mon; tour times change, so check website for the latest. As there is no box office, reserve at www.casalleomorera.com or in person at Palau de la Virreina cultural center (Ramblas 99, tel. 933-161-000, www.lavirreina.bcn.cat). The house itself is at Passeig de Gràcia 35. Tel. 936-762-733.

▲▲La Pedrera (Casa Milà)

One of Gaudí's trademark works, this house—built between 1906 and 1912—is an icon of Modernisme. The wealthy industrialist Pere Milà i Camps commissioned it, and while some still call it "Casa Milà," most call it La Pedrera (The Quarry) because of its jagged, rocky facade. It's worth going inside, as it's arguably the purest Gaudí interior in town—executed at the height of his abilities (unlike his earlier Palau Güell)—and still contains original furnishings.

The typical bourgeois **apartment** you'll visit is decorated as it might have been by its first middle-class urbanites (a seven-minute video explains Barcelona society at the time). Notice Gaudí's clever use of the atrium to maximize daylight.

In the **attic,** under parabola-shaped arches that support the roof, a sprawling multimedia exhibit traces the architect's career. Finally you reach the undulating, jaw-dropping **rooftop** and fine views. (Make sure you budget enough time to enjoy the roof, and note that it may close when it rains.) Explore this forest of playful, sculpted towers, where 30 chimneys play volleyball with the clouds.

▶ €20.50. Open daily March-Oct 9:00-20:00, Nov-Feb 9:00-18:30. Good audioguide-€4. Located at the corner of Passeig de Gràcia and Provença, at Provença 261, Metro: Diagonal. Info tel. 902-400-973, www.lapedrera.com.

Avoiding Lines: Avoid a wait (up to 1.5 hours) by reserving an assigned entry time at www.lapedrera.com. If you come without a ticket, the best time to arrive is right when it opens.

Free Entrance to Atrium: The door directly on the corner leads to the main atrium and, upstairs on the first floor, temporary exhibits. There's a café on the mezzanine level.

Nighttime Visits: Pricey after-hours visits (generally at 21:15), *dubbed "The Secret Pedrera," include a guided tour with the lights down low and a glass of cava. On summer weekends, La Pedrera hosts a rooftop concert series.*

▲▲▲Sagrada Família (Holy Family Church)

Antoni Gaudí's grand masterpiece sits unfinished in a residential Eixample neighborhood 1.5 miles north of Plaça de Catalunya. Its soaring spires and melting-in-the-rain facades are an icon of the city.

⚙ See the Sagrada Família Tour chapter.

Beyond the Eixample

▲▲Park Güell

Tucked in the foothills at the northwest edge of Barcelona, this fanciful park—designed by Antoni Gaudí—combines playful design, inviting public spaces, and sweeping views. Begun in 1900, it was intended to be a gated community for Barcelona's *nouveaux riches,* including the developer Eusebi Güell (pronounced "gway"). With World War I, progress stalled, and the place became a park. Much of the park is free, but the "Monumental Zone," with the iconic Gaudí features—the trademark dragon, tiled stairway, wavy benches, view terrace, and more—has an entry fee.

At the **main entrance,** walk through a palm-frond gate, past two Hansel-and-Gretel gingerbread houses that announce this is a magical space. (One house is a good bookshop; the other a skippable museum.)

Now climb the **main staircase.** The caves on either side were garages for Güell's newfangled automobiles. You'll pass the famous dragon fountain of St. George that's become an icon of the city.

Park Güell stairs to Hall of 100 Columns

Park Güell terrace has a great city view.

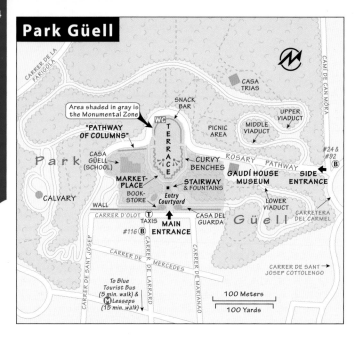

Park Güell

Area shaded in gray is the Monumental Zone

CARRER DE LA FARGOLA

CAMÍ DE CAN MÒRA

CASA TRIAS

SNACK BAR

UPPER VIADUCT

"PATHWAY OF COLUMNS"

WC

T E R R A C E

PICNIC AREA

MIDDLE VIADUCT

Park

CASA GÜELL (SCHOOL)

CURVY BENCHES

ROSARY PATHWAY

#24 & #92

B

MARKET-PLACE

STAIRWAY & FOUNTAINS

GAUDÍ HOUSE MUSEUM

SIDE ENTRANCE

CALVARY

BOOK-STORE

Entry Courtyard

LOWER VIADUCT

Güell

CARRETERA DEL CARMEL

WALL

CARRER D'OLOT

TAXIS

T

MAIN ENTRANCE

CASA DEL GUARDA

#116 B

CARRER DE SANT JOSEP

CARRER DE MERCEDES

CARRER DE LARRARD

CARRER DE MARIANAO

CARRER DE SANT → JOSEP COTTOLENGO

To Blue Tourist Bus (5 min. walk) & M Lesseps (15 min. walk)

100 Meters

100 Yards

At the top is the **Hall of 100 Columns** (actually 86), the produce market for the housing development. On the ceiling are four giant sun-like decorations (the four seasons), designed to hold lanterns from their hooks. Here and elsewhere are surfaces covered with Modernisme's signature *trencadís* mosaics—colorful bits of broken dishes and discarded tile. Though Gaudí became famous for the technique, most of this was executed by his collaborator, Josep Maria Jujol.

Continue up the left-hand staircase, looking left, down the playful **Pathway of Columns.** Gaudí drew his inspiration from nature, and this arcade is like a surfer's perfect tube. Gaudí intended for cars to travel across the top, with pedestrians in the arcade below.

Continuing up, you pop out on the **terrace.** Sit on the colorful, undulating, 360-foot-long bench and enjoy one of Barcelona's best views. (Find Gaudí's Sagrada Família church in the distance.) The terrace was to be the community's wide-open meeting place. Gaudí engineered a system to catch the terrace's rainwater runoff and funnel it down into a 300,000-gallon underground cistern. The water was bottled and sold; excess water powers the park's fountains.

The pink house with a steeple was Gaudí's home for the 20 years he worked here, though Gaudí did not design it. Today it's the **Gaudí House Museum** with some quirky Gaudí furniture.

The park's highest point is the **Calvary,** a stubby stone tower with three crosses representing the hill where Christ was crucified. Gaudí envisioned the topography of Park Güell as a spiritual journey—starting at the low end and toiling upward to reach spiritual enlightenment. If not enlightenment, the tower rewards you with a heavenly panorama of Barcelona.

▸ *Monumental Zone—€8 at the gate or €7 online, best to reserve timed-entry ticket in advance, daily April-Oct 8:00-20:00 (May-Aug until 21:30), Nov-March 8:30-18:15, www.parkguell.cat. Gaudí House Museum—€5.50, €18.50 combo-ticket with Sagrada Família (church but no towers), daily April-Sept 10:00-20:00, Oct-March 10:00-18:00, www. casamuseugaudi.org.*

The park is 2.5 miles from Plaça de Catalunya. It's easiest to take a taxi (about €12) or ride the blue Tourist Bus to the main entrance. From Plaça de Catalunya, public bus #24 travels to the park's side entrance.

Tibidabo

Barcelona's highest peak (1,600 feet), located five miles northwest of downtown, is topped with the city's oldest funfair (pricey but great for kids), and—if the weather and air quality are good—an almost limitless view of the city and the Mediterranean.

▸ *Get there by Metro, taxi, or the blue Tourist Bus. From the Tibidabo Metro station, catch a tram (the Tramvía Blau) to Plaça Dr. Andreu (€4.50 one-way), then take a funicular to the top (€7.70); www.tibidabo.cat.*

Montjuïc

Montjuïc (mohn-jew-EEK, "Mount of the Jews"), the hill overlooking Barcelona's hazy port, offers a park-like setting that's home to a variety of good (if not knockout) sights. You could lace together a number of them in a day of sightseeing, or just focus on one or two.

Getting to Montjuïc: A taxi costs about €8 from downtown. From Plaça de Catalunya, bus #55 goes as far as Montjuïc's cable-car station/

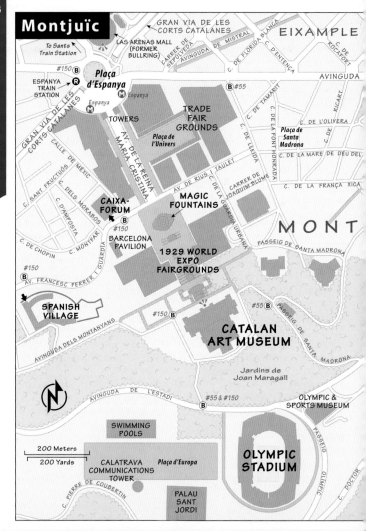

Montjuïc

GRAN VIA DE LES CORTS CATALANES

EIXAMPLE

C. DE ROCAFORT

To Sants Train Station

LAS ARENAS MALL (FORMER BULLRING)

CARRER DE SEPÚLVEDA

AVINGUDA DE MISTRAL

C. DE FLORIDA BLANCA

C. D'ENTENÇA

#150 B

Plaça d'Espanya

ESPANYA TRAIN STATION R

AVINGUDA

B #55

ESPANYA TRAIN STATION

Espanya M

M Espanya

TOWERS

TRADE FAIR GROUNDS

C. DE TAMARIT

C. DE L'OLIVERA

C. DE RICART

Plaça de Santa Madrona

GRAN VIA DE LES CORTS CATALANES

CALLE DE MÉXIC

C. SANT FRUCTUÓS

C. DELS MORABOS

Plaça de l'Univers

AV. DE LA REINA MARIA CRISTINA

C. DE LLEIDA

C. DE LA FONT HONRADA

C. DE LA MARE DE DÉU DEL

C. D'AMPOSTA

CAIXA-FORUM

B #150

AV. DE RIUS I TAULET

MAGIC FOUNTAINS

C. DE LA GUARDIA URBANA

CARRER DE JOAQUIM BLUME

C. DE LA FRANÇA XICA

MONT

BARCELONA PAVILION

C. DE CHOPIN

C. MONTFAR

B #150

AV. FRANCESC FERRER I GUÀRDIA

1929 WORLD EXPO FAIRGROUNDS

PASSEIG DE SANTA MADRONA

SPANISH VILLAGE

AVINGUDA DELS MONTANYANS

#150 B

B #55

PASSEIG DE SANTA MADRONA

CATALAN ART MUSEUM

Jardins de Joan Maragall

N

AVINGUDA DE L'ESTADI

#55 & #150 B

OLYMPIC & SPORTS MUSEUM

SWIMMING POOLS

C. DOCTOR

200 Meters

200 Yards

CALATRAVA COMMUNICATIONS TOWER

Plaça d'Europa

OLYMPIC STADIUM

C. PIERRE DE COUBERTIN

PALAU SANT JORDI

PASSEIG OLÍMPIC

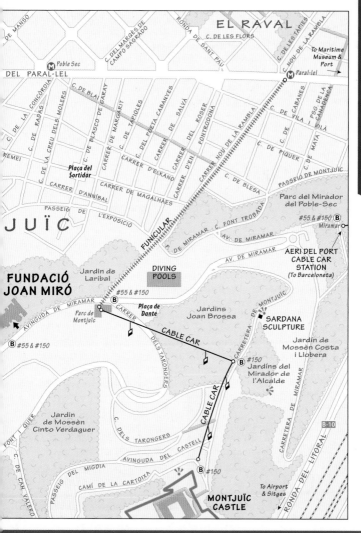

EL RAVAL

C. DE LES FLORS

To Maritime
Museum &
Port

Ⓜ Poble Sec

DEL PARAL-LEL

Ⓜ Paral-lel

C. DE BLAI

C. DE GARAY

C. DE BLASCO DE GARAY

C. DEL MARGÈS DE CAMPO SAGRADO

RONDA DE SANT PAU

C. DE LES TAPIES

C. NOU DE LA RAMBLA

C. DE CABANES

PSG. DE LA CANADENCA

C. DE VILA I VILA

C. DE LA CONCÒRDIA

C. DE RADAS

C. DE LA CREU DELS MOLERS

C. DE MARGARIT

C. DEL POETA CABANYES

C. DE SALVÀ

CARRER DEL ROSER

C. D'EN FONTRODONA

C. DE MATA

C. DE PIQUER

Plaça del Sortidor

CARRER D'ELKANO

CARRER NOU DE LA RAMBLA

C. DE BLESA

PASSEIG DE MONTJUÏC

C. DEL REMEI

CARRER DE MAGALHÃES

CARRER DE MAGALHÃES

CARRER D'ANNIBAL

PASSEIG DE L'EXPOSICIÓ

Parc del Mirador del Poble-Sec

JUÏC

FUNICULAR

P. DE MIRAMAR

C. FONT TROBADA

AV. DE MIRAMAR

#55 & #150 Ⓑ
Miramar

AV. DE MIRAMAR

DIVING POOLS

AERI DEL PORT CABLE CAR STATION
(To Barceloneta)

FUNDACIÓ JOAN MIRÓ

Jardin de Laribal

AVINGUDA DE MIRAMAR

Ⓑ #55 & #150

Parc de Montjuïc

CARRER DELS TARONGERS

Plaça de Dante

CABLE CAR

Jardins Joan Brossa

CARRETERA DE MONTJUÏC

SARDANA SCULPTURE

Ⓑ #55 & #150

Ⓑ #150
Jardíns del Mirador de l'Alcalde

Jardin de Mossèn Costa i Llobera

CABLE CAR

CARRETERA DE MIRAMAR

Jardin de Mossèn Cinto Verdaguer

C. DELS TARONGERS

FONT I GUER

C. DE CAN VALERO

PASSEIG DEL MIGDIA

AVINGUDA DEL CASTELL

CAMÍ DE LA CARTOIXA

Ⓑ #150

B-10

RONDA DEL LITORAL

To Airport & Sitges

MONTJUÏC CASTLE

funicular. To get higher (to the castle), ride the Metro or bus #9 or #50 from Plaça de Catalunya to Plaça d'Espanya, then transfer to bus #150. The red Tourist Bus also swings by the main sights. A funicular (covered by Metro ticket) goes up from the Paral-lel Metro stop. From the top of the funicular, you can walk to several sights, or catch a cable car up to the castle (€7.80 one-way, €11.50 round-trip; another cable car line, from the tip of the Barceloneta peninsula, is scenic but ex-cru-ci-a-ting-ly slow). If you only want to go to the base of the hill (Catalan Art Museum and CaixaForum), you can ride the escalators from Plaça d'Espanya.

Getting Around Montjuïc: The various sights are (more or less) a quarter-mile apart. It's easy to walk between them along streets and paths—especially downhill. You can also connect the sights using the red Tourist Bus, public bus #150, or bus #55 (though it skips the castle). To see all the sights, ride up to the castle (by taxi, bus, or funicular/cable car), then walk or ride downhill, seeing them in the order below.

Castle of Montjuïc (Castell de Montjuïc)

While just an empty brick-and-concrete shell today, the castle offers great city views from its ramparts. It was built in the 18th century by the central Spanish government to keep an eye on rebellious Barcelona. Survey the Mediterranean and the boats in the harbor: container ships, ferries to Mallorca, and cruise ships. To the left is the former industrial zone that's now a swanky stretch of beaches and fancy condos. To the right is Spain's leading port; you'll see containers stretching all the way to the airport.

▸ *€5. Open daily 10:00-20:00, until 18:00 Nov-March. To get there, take a taxi, bus #150 from Plaça d'Espanya, or the funicular-plus-cable car from Metro: Paral-lel; www.bcn.cat/castelldemontjuic.*

Fundació Joan Miró, on Montjuïc

550-foot Montjuïc overlooks the harbor.

▲ Fundació Joan Miró

This is the best collection anywhere of work by the pioneering abstract artist Joan Miró (1893-1983). It's an always-changing, loosely chronological overview of Miró's oeuvre, plus excellent temporary exhibits.

Born in Barcelona, Miró divided his time between Paris and Catalunya. His style is simple, with shapes that suggest the basic elements of the cosmos—things like stars, people, music, love. To appreciate Miró's art, try this: Meditate on it, then read the title (for example, *The Smile of a Tear*), then meditate again. Rinse and repeat until you have an epiphany. There's no correct answer—it's pure poetry.

The permanent collection starts on the main floor. Room 11 has the 400-square-foot *Tapestry of the Foundation* (1979) that Miró designed for this space. Notice his trademark star and moon. Nearby, detour downstairs for a 15-minute film about Miró.

Room 16 traces young Miró's artistic development as he experiments with Fauvism, Cubism, Catalan folk art, and Impressionism. In 1920, he traveled to Paris, dabbled in Dada, and socialized with Surrealists. Like them, Miró's work tries to circumvent the viewer's preconceptions by juxtaposing unlikely images in order to short-circuit the brain. His Green Paintings (1925-1927) became increasingly abstract, replacing photo-realistic images with abstract symbols on a flat background. By 1925, Miró was leaving the figurative world behind, painting a completely abstract, uninterpretable canvas, cheekily titled "*Painting*."

Head upstairs to the second floor. With the advent of the Spanish Civil War, Miró temporarily revived his figurative style to depict the monsters of war (Wind Paintings, 1930s). In the 1940s, he became fixated on the heavens, producing his Constellations series, featuring colorful stars and moons on bright backgrounds. The Sixties Gallery shows him refining his signature style, stripping everything down to the basics. Star. Moon. Bird. Woman.

Some of Miró's best work can't be found in any museum—it's scattered around the streets of Barcelona, including the center of the Ramblas (✪ see page 27).

▶ *€11. Open Tue-Sat 10:00-20:00 (until 19:00 Oct-June), Thu until 21:00, Sun 10:00-14:30, closed Mon. Great €5 audioguide. Located 200 yards from top of funicular. Tel. 934-439-470, www.fundaciomiro-bcn.org.*

Olympic Stadium of 1929 and 1992 Games

The Catalan Art Museum has medieval frescoes.

Olympic Stadium (Estadi Olímpic) and Olympic and Sports Museum (Museu Olímpic i de l'Esport)

Barcelona's Olympic Stadium offers little to see today, but if the doors are open, you're welcome to step inside. Originally built for the 1929 World Expo, the stadium was updated for the 1992 Summer Olympics. At the opening ceremonies, an archer dramatically lit the Olympic torch—which still stands high—with a flaming arrow. This was the Olympics of the US basketball "Dream Team" (Michael Jordan and company), and the first after the fall of the Soviet Union. The futuristic communications tower is by the famous Spanish architect Santiago Calatrava.

Next door, at the Sports Museum, you'll twist down a timeline-ramp that traces the history of the Olympic Games. Downstairs, you'll find exhibits that test your athleticism, remember the '92 Olympiad, and honor Juan Antonio Samaranch, the influential Catalan president of the IOC for two decades. High-tech but hokey, the museum is worth it only for those nostalgic for the '92 Games.

▶ €5.10. Open April-Sept Tue-Sat 10:00-20:00 (until 18:00 Oct-March), Sun 10:00-14:30, closed Mon. Located at Avinguda de l'Estadi 60. Tel. 932-925-379, www.museuolimpicbcn.cat.

▲▲Catalan Art Museum (Museu Nacional d'Art de Catalunya)

The "MNAC" is often called "the Prado of Romanesque art" for its world-class medieval frescoes. It's also a sweep through Catalan art from the 10th to the 20th century. For art aficionados, this is a major sight.

The Romanesque art (in the left wing of the museum) came mostly from remote Catalan village churches high in the Pyrenees. You'll see frescoes, statues, and painted wooden altar fronts—with flat 2-D scenes, each saint holding his symbol, and Jesus with his cross-shaped halo—all displayed in replica church settings.

The Gothic murals (right wing) evolve into vivid 14th-century wood-panel paintings of Bible stories. Don't miss the Catalan master Jaume Huguet (1412-1492) and his *Consecration of St. Agustí Vell* (in Room 26).

Upstairs, the Renaissance and Modern Art section covers Spain's Golden Age—Zurbarán, heavy religious scenes, Spanish royals with their endearing underbites, and Romanticism. In the Modern section, circle clockwise for a short chronological tour through Symbolism, Modernisme, Art Deco, and more. Catalan artist Ramon Casas (and his Toulouse-Lautrec-esque works) had a profound impact on young Picasso. In the "Modern 2" section, you'll find Modernist-era furniture, Impressionism, and several distinctly Picasso portraits of women.

The museum also has a coin collection and the chic and pricey Oleum restaurant, with vast city views.

▶ *€12, free every Sat from 15:00 and all day on first Sun of month, rooftop access only-€3.50. Open Tue-Sat 10:00-20:00 (until 18:00 Oct-April), Sun 10:00-15:00, closed Mon. Located above the Magic Fountains near Plaça d'Espanya—take the escalators up. Tel. 936-220-376, www.mnac.cat.*

▲World Expo Fairgrounds, Plaça d'Espanya, and More

Stretching from Plaça d'Espanya to the base of Montjuïc, this sprawling cluster of buildings, fountains, plazas, and esplanades was originally built for the 1929 World Expo. Today it's part of an impressive neighborhood of old and new buildings that create some wonderful public spaces. It's worth a visit for its architecture (Modernista, Art Deco, and Modern), and for glimpses into Barcelona today. It's free to stroll the grounds, starting either from Plaça d'Espanya (convenient Metro stop) or as you descend from Montjuïc.

▲Magic Fountains (Font Màgica):
Music, colored lights, and huge amounts of water make an artistic splash many evenings.

▶ *Free 20-minute shows start on the half-hour, almost always May-Sept Thu-Sun 21:00-23:00, no shows Mon-Wed; Oct-April Fri-Sat 19:00-20:30, no shows Sun-Thu. From the Espanya Metro stop, walk toward the towering National Palace.*

World Expo Fairgrounds, Plaça d'Espanya   Las Arenas—bullring turned shopping mall

▲▲**CaixaForum:** One of Barcelona's most important Art Nouveau buildings—by Josep Puig i Cadafalch (✪ see page 87)—was built as a state-of-the-art textile factory. In 2002, it reopened as a cultural center, bringing art to the people for free. Ride the escalator to the first floor for a permanent display about the building, then explore the temporary exhibits. The Modernista Terrace boasts a wavy floor, bristling with fanciful brick towers, and offers great views. Across the street is the Mies van der Rohe Pavilion, an austere building that demonstrates the stripped-down, strictly functional "Modernist" architecture (i.e., decidedly not "Modernista").

▶ *Free to enter building, €4 for exhibits. Open daily 10:00-20:00. Avinguda de Francesc Ferrer i Guàrdia 6. Tel. 934-768-600, http://obrasocial. lacaixa.es—click on "Culture."*

Spanish Village (Poble Espanyol): A tacky and overpriced five-acre faux village (complete with craftspeople selling trinkets), built for the 1929 World Expo to show off the "real" Spain.

▶ *€12. Open daily 10:00-20:00 or later, closes earlier off-season. Avinguda de Francesc Ferrer i Guàrdia 13, Metro: Espanya. Tel. 935-086-300, www.poble-espanyol.com.*

▲**Las Arenas (Bullring Mall):** What do you do with a big arena that's been sitting empty for decades? Make a mall. The former bullfight ring now hosts brand-name shops, a food-circus basement, a multiplex, a rock-and-roll museum, and a roof terrace with stupendous views of Plaça d'Espanya and Montjuïc (reachable by external glass elevator for €1 or from inside for free).

▶ *Free. Open daily 10:00-22:00. Gran Via de les Corts Catalanes 373, Metro: Espanya, www.arenasdebarcelona.com.*

Day Trips

Three sights are day-trip temptations from Barcelona.

Montserrat: The "serrated mountain" rockets dramatically up from the valley floor northwest of Barcelona. With its unique rock formations, a dramatic mountaintop monastery (also called Montserrat), and spiritual connection with the Catalan people and their struggles, it's a popular day trip (tour groups mob the place at midday and on Sundays). You can see the Sacred Cave (where, in medieval times, some shepherd children found a Black Virgin statue), visit the Basilica (where the statue is venerated today), wander meditative trails, and stop into a small museum of sacred art.

▶ *Getting There: From Barcelona's Plaça d'Espanya (the FGC underground station), take train line R5 (1.5 hours, direction: Manresa) to the Montserrat-Aeri Station at the base of the mountain, where you can catch the scenic cable car (closed during lunchtime, www.aerideemontserrat. com). You can pay as you go or—smarter—buy combo-tickets (at Plaça de Catalunya TI or Plaça de Espanya train station) that cover the train, cable car, and admission to sights (packages range from €23-47).*

Figueres: Two hours by train from Barcelona, the town of Figueres (feeg-YEHR-ehs) is only of interest for its world-class Salvador Dalí Theater-Museum. It's an outrageously fun collection of work by the town's native son, the master Surrealist Salvador Dalí (1904-1989). True Dalí fans will continue another hour north of Figueres by bus to the sleepy fishing village of Cadaqués to visit the artist's family cabin, called the Salvador Dalí House.

▶ *Getting There: Trains to Figueres depart hourly from Barcelona's Sants Station or from the RENFE station at Metro: Passeig de Gràcia.*

The Dalí Theater-Museum (Teatre-Museu Dalí) in Figueres (€12) is open July-Sept daily 9:00-20:00; shorter hours and closed Mon off-season; last entry 45 minutes before closing. Tel. 972-677-500, www. salvador-dali.org.

The Salvador Dalí House in Cadaqués (€11) requires an advance reservation. Tel. 972-251-015, www.salvador-dali.org.

Sitges: For the consummate day at the beach, head 40 minutes south of Barcelona to this charming, artsy, and free-spirited resort town. Today's Sitges (SEE-juhz) is a world-renowned vacation destination among the gay community. With a pleasant Old Town and fine beaches, it's a great break from the big city.

▶ *Getting There: From Barcelona's Sants Station or the Passeig de Gràcia RENFE station, take the Rodalies train on the dark-green line R2 toward Sant Vincenç de Calders.*

Sleeping

I favor hotels that are close to the sightseeing action: near Plaça de Catalunya, the Ramblas, the Barri Gòtic, and the Eixample.

I like places that are clean, small, central, relatively quiet at night (except for the buzz of the neighborhood), traditional, inexpensive, family-run, friendly, and not listed in other guidebooks. A hotel with six out of these nine attributes is a keeper.

Double rooms listed in this book average around €125 (including a private bathroom), ranging from a low of roughly €60 (very simple, with toilet and shower down the hall) to €300 (modern rooms and chandeliered lobbies).

Although Spain has some of Western Europe's best hotel rates, Barcelona is Spain's most expensive city. Book ahead and look for

Hotel Price Code

$$$ Most rooms are €150 or more.
$$ Most rooms between €100-150.
$ Most rooms €100 or less.

These rates are for a standard double room with bath during high season. Unless otherwise noted, hotels have an elevator and air-conditioning, and Wi-Fi is generally free. Many hotels charge extra for breakfast. Prices listed may not include the 10 percent IVA hotel tax or the €1-2 per person, per night tourist tax.

discounts (see "Budget Tips," next page). Hotel prices can fluctuate wildly from day-to-day and season-to season. It's hard to identify firm prices—I've assigned price codes based on an average price. On the plus side, bargain-hunters can find some great deals.

A Typical Barcelona Hotel

A €125 double room in Barcelona is small by American standards and has one double bed or two twins. There's probably a bathroom in the room with a toilet, sink, and bathtub or shower. Rooms generally have a telephone and TV, and may have a safe. Most hotels at this price will have elevators and air-conditioning—cheaper places may not. (Travelers in spring and fall should prepare for hoteliers who may be stingy turning on the heat or air-conditioning.) Some rooms have a small fridge stocked with drinks for sale.

Breakfast is generally offered for an additional €5-15. It can range from a simple roll and coffee to a self-service buffet of cereal, ham, cheese, yogurt, and juice.

Nearly all hotels have some form of Internet access, likely free or with a small charge. It may be Wi-Fi in your room or a guest computer in the lobby. The staff speaks at least enough English to get by. Night clerks aren't paid enough to care deeply about problems that arise. If you have issues, ask to see the complaint book *(libro de reclamaciones);* the request alone will generally prompt the hotelier to solve your problem.

Since Barcelona parties late, street noise can be a problem, especially in cheap places with single-pane windows. You may have to choose between an atmospheric room with a view *(con vista)* or a quiet room in back *(tranquilo)*.

Making Reservations

Barcelona is the rare big city that doesn't empty out in summer, with high season *(temporada alta)* extending from July to September. Shoulder season *(temporada media)* is roughly April through June and October. Low season *(temporada baja)* runs from November through March. Barcelona's many festivals raise rates to peak-season levels.

Make reservations by phone, through the hotel's website, or with an email that reads something like this:

Dear Hotel Barcelona,
I would like to reserve a double room for 2 people for 3 nights, arriving 19 July and departing 22 July. If possible, I would like a quiet room with a double bed (not twin beds), a city view, and a shower (not a tub). Please let me know if you have a room available and the price. Thank you.

If the hotel requires your credit-card number for a deposit, you can send it by email (I do), but it's safer via phone, the hotel's secure website, or split between two emails. Once your room is booked, print out the confirmation, and reconfirm your reservation with a phone call or email a day or two in advance. If you must cancel your reservation, hotels require advance notice or you'll be billed. Even if there's no penalty, it's polite to give at least three days' notice.

Budget Tips

Some of my listed hotels offer special rates to my readers—it's worth asking when you reserve your room.

Barcelona hotel rates can change from day to day. To get the best rates, book directly with the hotel, not through a hotel-booking engine. Start with the hotel's website, looking for promo deals. Check rates every few days, as prices can vary greatly based on demand. Email several hotels to ask for their best price and compare offers—you may be astonished at the range. You may get a better rate if you offer to pay cash, stay at least three nights, skip breakfast, or simply ask if there are any cheaper rooms.

Sleeping

Rates can be sky-high during festivals and drop off-season—roughly November through March.

Big expensive hotels are most apt to mark down rooms. You might snag a €200 double for €100 by booking through a big hotel's website. At these business-class places, discounts are most likely—surprisingly—on weekends and in summer. (Conversely, less-expensive hotels are usually most crowded on weekends and in summer.) Given the economic downturn, hoteliers are eager to deal rather than let a room go empty.

In addition to hotels, I also list a few alternatives. The words *hostal* and *pension* designate cheap family-owned hotels. These may not have plush lobbies and modern amenities, but you'll get a fully private hotel room. I also recommend a few hostels *(albergue juvenil),* where you can rent a dorm-style bed for around €25 (for more listings see www.hostelworld.com, www.hihostels.com, or Barcelona's excellent Equity Point Hostels—tel. 932-312-045, www.equity-point.com).

Renting an apartment can be a good value (around €100/day) for those who stay a week and do their own cooking. Airbnb.com makes it reasonably easy to find a place to sleep in someone's home, or try a booking agency like Cross-Pollinate (US tel. 800-270-1190, www.cross-pollinate.com, info@cross-pollinate.com). Or you can try a local rental agency, such as Top Barcelona Apartments (http://top-barcelona-apartments.com) or MH Apartments (www.mhapartments.com).

Don't be too cheap when picking a hotel in Barcelona. In this big, bustling, 24/7 city, it's nice to have a pleasant oasis to call home.

NEAR PLAÇA DE CATALUNYA—Convenient location, plush lobbies, air-con, elevators, sterile modern rooms, and fluctuating prices (I've listed the average but always ask for a deal, especially on weekends and in summer); Metro: Catalunya or Universitat

$$$ Hotel Catalonia Plaça Catalunya Carrer de Bergara 11 | tel. 933-015-151 www.hoteles-catalonia.com	Four-star elegance, posh lobby, garden courtyard, comfortable but simple rooms, a world away from big-city noise
$$ Hotel Denit Carrer d'Estruc 24 | tel. 935-454-000 www.denit.com	36-room hotel on pedestrian street; chic, minimalist, and fun; rooms priced by size (small, XL, etc.)
$$ Hotel Inglaterra Carrer de Pelai 14 | tel. 935-051-100 www.hotel-inglaterra.com	60 rooms, rooftop terrace, small swimming pool, free breakfast if you book through their website
$$ Hotel Reding Carrer de Gravina 5 | tel. 934-121-097 www.hotelreding.com	10-minute walk west of Plaça, on quiet street, sleek place with 44 mod rooms at reasonable price
$$ Hotel Lleó Carrer de Pelai 22 | tel. 933-181-312 www.hotel-lleo.com	The "YAH-oh" is well-run with 92 big, bright, comfortable rooms; good public spaces, small rooftop pool
$$ Hotel Atlantis Carrer de Pelai 20 | tel. 933-189-012 www.hotelatlantis-bcn.com	50 big, nondescript, modern rooms, fair price for the location
$ Hotel Ginebra Rambla de Catalunya 1 tel. 932-502-017 www.barcelonahotelginebra.com	Renovated, modern, fresh version of an old-school *pension* in classic building on corner of Plaça de Catalunya

ON OR NEAR THE RAMBLAS—Generally family-run, with ad-lib furnishings, more character, and lower prices; Metro: Catalunya or Liceu

$$ Hotel Continental Barcelona Ramblas 138 | tel. 933-012-570 www.hotelcontinental.com	Tiny-balcony rooms with Ramblas views and noise, quieter back rooms, comfortable but faded, free snacks
$$ Hostería Grau Ramelleres 27 | tel. 933-018-135 www.hostalgrau.com	Homey, family-run, cheery rooms, away from Ramblas in colorful university district, strict cancellation policy

Sleeping

$ Hostal el Jardí Plaça Sant Josep Oriol 1 tel. 933-015-900 www.eljardi-barcelona.com	Clean, tight, and plain rooms; petite view balconies, ambience of quaint Barri Gòtic square (but you're paying for it), book early
$ Hostal Operaramblas Carrer de Sant Pau 20 | tel. 933-188-201 www.operaramblas.com	Just off Ramblas; simple, clean, institutional, modern rooms; semi-seedy at night but safe, great value

IN THE OLD CITY—Buried in an atmospheric, tight tangle of lanes; Metro: Liceu, Jaume I, or Catalunya

$$$ Hotel Neri Carrer de Sant Sever 5 tel. 933-040-655 www.hotelneri.com	Posh, pretentious, and sophisticated; on small square near cathedral, modern art, high-class service
$$$ NH Hotel Barcelona Centro Carrer del Duc 15 | tel. 932-703-410 www.nh-hotels.com	156-room chain hotel, predictably professional yet friendly, three blocks off Ramblas
$$$ Hotel Nouvel Carrer de Santa Anna 20 tel. 933-018-274 www.hotelnouvel.com	Victorian-style building with character on handy pedestrian street, royal lounges, 78 comfy rooms
$$ Hotel Banys Orientals Carrer de l'Argenteria 37 tel. 932-688-460 www.hotelbanysorientals.com	Modern boutique hotel with people-to-people ethic, 43 restful rooms, on pedestrian street in El Born
$$ Hotel Racó del Pi Carrer del Pi 7 | tel. 933-426-190 www.h10hotels.com	Chain hotel on colorful Barri Gòtic lane; 37 bright, quiet, modern rooms; big lobby
$$ Hotel Regencia Colón Carrer dels Sagristans 13 tel. 933-189-858 www.hotelregenciacolon.com	One block from cathedral, 50 older but solid, classy, well-priced rooms
$ Gothic Point Hostel Carrer Vigatans 5 | tel. 932-687-808 www.gothicpoint.com	130 dorm-style beds, a block from Picasso Museum, roof terrace

IN THE EIXAMPLE—Uptown, boulevard-like neighborhood; 10-minute walk to the Ramblas; Metro: Catalunya, Passeig de Gràcia, or Urquinaona

$$ Hotel Granvía Gran Via de les Corts Catalanes 642 tel. 933-181-900 www.hotelgranvia.com	Mansion with 58 bright, spacious rooms; peaceful sun patio, comfortable common areas
$$ Hotel Continental Palacete 30 Rambla de Catalunya tel. 934-457-657 www.hotelcontinental.com	19 small rooms in mansion with flowery wallpaper; friendly, quiet, and well-located; outdoor terrace, free buffet
$ Hostal Oliva Passeig de Gràcia 32 | tel. 934-880-162 www.hostaloliva.com	Spartan old-school place in classic old building, 15 basic and bright rooms, no breakfast or lobby, good location
$ BCN Fashion House B&B Carrer del Bruc 13 | mobile 637-904-044 www.bcnfashionhouse.com	Small, meditative place; 10 basic rooms, peaceful lounge, leafy backyard terrace, in nondescript old building
$ Centric Point Hostel Passeig de Gràcia 33 | tel. 932-151-796 www.centricpointhostel.com	Huge place renting 400 cheap dorm beds in upscale location
$ Somnio Hostel Carrer de la Diputació 251, second floor tel. 932-725-308 www.somniohostels.com	Small, innovative, American-run place with 10 simple, clean rooms

Eating

Barcelona, the capital of Catalan cuisine, offers a tremendous variety of colorful places to eat. Elbowing up to a lively bar for appetizers, then lingering over a late meal in a classy restaurant...these are some of Barcelona's great pleasures.

In general, Barcelona's eateries rise to a higher level than elsewhere in Spain, propelled by talented chefs who aren't afraid to experiment, the relative affluence, and the availability of good, fresh ingredients—especially fish and seafood.

I list a full range of options—from workaday eateries to homey Catalan bistros (cans) to crowded tapas bars to avant-garde restaurants. In fact, many fall somewhere in between a restaurant and bar, serving both stand-up tapas and sit-down meals. My recommendations are near the Ramblas (working-class places amid the tourists), the Barri Gòtic (atmospheric lanes and squares), El Born (trendy bistros), and the modern, upscale Eixample.

Restaurant Price Code

$$$ Most main courses €15 or more
$$ Most main courses €10-15.
$ Most main courses €10 or less.

Based on the average price of a meat or seafood dish (a main dish) on the menu. For tapas places, I've used the price of a racion. So a typical meal in a $$ restaurant—including appetizer, main dish, house wine, water, and service charge—would cost about €30. The circled numbers in the restaurant listings indicate locations on the maps on ✪ pages 154-157.

Eating on the Spanish Schedule

When in Barcelona, I eat on the local schedule. Breakfast (at the hotel or a corner bar) is little more than a roll and coffee. Around 11:00, many Spaniards grab a quick sandwich to tide them over. Lunch (*comida*), around 14:00, is the major meal of the day, a social event enjoyed with friends and family. Dinner (*cena*) is light and eaten very late—after 21:00. At any time of day, Spaniards snack by popping into casual bars for tapas and drinks.

Dining Out

Barcelona's restaurants can be divided into two types: sit-down restaurants and tapas bars. At restaurants, meal times are late and portions are generous if not quite American-sized. Tapas bars serve small plates (either sit-down or stand-up) throughout the afternoon and evening. While finer tapas bars can provide a serious dining option with a small-plates-style menu, formal restaurants don't offer tapas—and they start their service much later than the American norm.

When dining out, take your schedule into consideration. If you want to eat early (American time), go to a tapas bar. Because the big meal is lunch (from the siesta heritage), people work a little later and have a smaller supper. That's one reason tapas are such a hit for locals in the evening.

If you're holding out for a restaurant, the earliest you can go is about 20:30, when the place is empty or filled with tourists. Going after 21:00

is better, but if you wait until 22:00, it can be hard to get into popular restaurants.

In basic restaurants and bars, you'll often find daily lunch specials (*menú del día*) for €10 to €12. And you can always graze cheaply in bars offering an array of affordable tapas. Formal restaurants have a standard à la carte menu. Many tapas bars are a combination of restaurant and bar—with some tables in the back or outside on the *terraza*. These combo places are likely to serve larger *raciones* (dinner plate-sized serving) rather than bite-size tapas.

In any tapas bar, couples or small groups typically order a few *raciones* and share the plates family-style. This can be very economical if you don't over-order. Remember this is informal, social eating. There's nothing wrong with ordering a tapa or two to start before deciding whether to continue in the same bar or at all.

Service is often *serio*—it's not friendly or unfriendly...just proficient. Ask for the bill in Catalan by saying *"El compte?"* Tipping is not a big concern here. Locals generally don't tip if ordering at the bar. For table service, most Spaniards skip the tip if service is included in the bill; you can round up 5 percent or so if the service was exceptional. ✪ For hints on tipping, see page 161.

If ordering mineral water, it's economical to request a *botella grande de agua* (big bottle). They push the more profitable small bottles. For a glass of tap water, specify *un vaso de agua del grifo.* Note that tap water in Barcelona, while perfectly safe, doesn't taste particularly good; some bar owners are rather insistent on not serving it to their clientele.

While the menu is usually in Spanish and Catalan, you may find menus in Catalan and English without Spanish. In any Catalan bar or restaurant, an occasional *si us plau* (please) or *moltes gràcies* (thank you very much) will go a long way with the locals, who are extremely proud of their language, history, and culture. An *adéu* (good-bye), *que vagi bé* (have a good one!) or, in the evening, *bona nit* (good evening/night) on your way out the door will certainly earn you a smile.

Sandwich shops are everywhere, serving made-to-order *bocadillos*. Choose between bright (mass-produced) chains such as Bocatta and Pans & Company, or colorful holes-in-the-wall. Mucci's Pizza has good, fresh, €2 pizza slices and empanadas, and Wok to Walk has takeaway noodle and rice dishes. Kebab places are another standby for quick and tasty €3-4 meals. For a fast, affordable lunch with a view, the ninth-floor cafeteria at El Corte Inglés department store on Plaça de Catalunya can't be beat. Picnickers can buy groceries at the basement supermarket in El Corte Inglés, or at La Boqueria Market on the Ramblas (✪ see page 24).

Tapas Bars

You can eat well any time of day in tapas bars. Tapas are small portions of seafood, salads, meat-filled pastries, deep-fried tasties, and on and on. There are several kinds of tapas bars: Traditional Spanish-style bars serve dishes in portions called *raciones,* or the smaller half-servings, *media-raciones,* that allow you to better sample a variety of the regional cuisine. Two people can fill up on four *media-raciones.*

Basque-style tapas bars lay the food out on the countertop. These tapas are called *pintxos* (or *pinchos*) and are wildly popular in Barcelona. (Remember to save the toothpicks so they know how many *pintxos* you've had when it's time to pay.) There are also traditional Catalan tapas bars and *bodegas* (originally denoting wine cellars but today also used for restaurants). Catalan tapas menus typically include more seafood, delicious local olives, and a traditional sausage called *butifarra.* All this food is accompanied by local beers, wines, and, of course, the beloved sweet vermouth. Part of the joy of eating at tapas bars is that you can make it a mobile feast, visiting two or three bars during a single meal.

Tapas typically cost €2 apiece and up. Some bars charge less if you stand or grab a stool at the bar and around 20 percent more if you sit at a table or on the terrace. I look for a small, official-looking menu (generally posted somewhere near the cashier) to see the drink options and the price difference between the *barra* (bar), the *mesa* or *salón* (indoor tables), and the *terraza* (outdoor tables).

If you're standing and a table opens up, it's OK to move as long as you signal to the waiter; anything else you order will be charged at the higher *mesa/salón* price. In the right place, a quiet snack and drink on a terrace on the town square is well worth the small extra charge. But the cheapest seats sometimes get the best show. Sit at the bar and study your bartender—he's an artist.

The authentic tapas experience can be intimidating: squeezing up to a bar crowded with pushy locals, squinting at a hand-scrawled, monolingual chalkboard menu, and trying to communicate with the brusque bartender. Your bartender isn't a "waiter" in any sense. He's not there to patiently help you sort through your options—he wants to take your order, period. Hang back and observe before ordering.

When you're ready to order, be assertive. *Si us plau* (please) or *perdó* (excuse me) grabs the server's attention. Then quickly rattle off what you'd like (pointing to other people's food if necessary). Don't worry about paying until you're ready to leave (he's keeping track of your tab).

Although tapas are served throughout the day, the real action begins late—21:00 at the earliest. For beginners, an earlier start is easier and comes with less commotion. Chasing down a particular bar nearly defeats the purpose and spirit of tapas. Just drop in at any lively place.

Eating

Survival Tips

Although some bars have a dizzying array of fancy tapas, even humble establishments will likely have some of these items. Where they differ greatly, I've given both the Spanish and Catalan terms.

Bocadillo (bocata)—A sandwich on baguette bread. The most popular is a *bocadillo de jamón* (ham).

Café con leche (café amb llet)—Coffee with hot milk

Zumo de naranja natural—Freshly squeezed orange juice

Tortilla española (truita de patata)—Potato omelet, often served at breakfast

Ensaladilla rusa—Potato salad with lots of mayo, peas, and carrots

Patatas bravas—Fried potatoes with spicy tomato sauce

Jamón (pernil)—Cured ham (like prosciutto)

Queso manchego (formatge manxec)—Classic Spanish sheep-milk cheese

Pimientos de Padrón—Fried green peppers, mostly mild but with the occasional Russian-roulette hot one

Catalan Cuisine

Cod, hake, tuna, squid, and anchovies appear on many menus, and you'll see Catalan favorites such as *fideuà,* a thin, flavor-infused noodle served with seafood—a kind of Catalan paella—and *arròs negre,* black rice cooked in squid ink. *Pa amb tomàquet* is the classic Catalan way to eat your bread—toasted white bread with olive oil, tomato, and a pinch of salt. It's often served with tapas and used to make sandwiches.

Catalan cuisine can be a bit heavy for Americans more accustomed to salads, fruits, and grains. The secret to getting your veggies at restaurants is to order two courses, because the first course generally has a green option. Resist the cheese-and-ham appetizers and instead choose first-course menu items such as creamed vegetable soup, *parrillada de verduras* (sautéed vegetables), or *ensalada mixta*. (Salads tend to be small and simple—just iceberg lettuce, tomatoes, and maybe olives and tuna.)

While the famous cured *jamón* (ham) is not as typically Catalan as it is Spanish, you'll still find lots of it in Catalunya. Another popular Spanish dish is the empanada—a pastry turnover filled with seasoned meat and vegetables. The cheapest meal is a simple *bocadillo de jamón* (ham sandwich on a baguette), sold virtually everywhere.

Those with a sweet tooth will find various sweet rolls (*bollos* or *bollería*). The familiar croissant, called a *palmera* (palm-shaped), is often coated in chocolate. A *caracol* ("snail"-shaped) is sometimes similar to a cinnamon roll. A *napolitana* is a rolled pastry, usually filled with chocolate or with a custard-like cream. If you like a doughnut and coffee in American greasy-spoon joints, try the Spanish equivalent: greasy, cigar-shaped fritters called *churros* (*xurros* in Catalan) or the thicker *porras*. Dip them in warm chocolate pudding or your *café con leche*.

No Spanish meal is complete without a drink. Spain produces lots of excellent wines—red *(tinto)* and white *(blanco)*. Major wine regions include Valdepeñas and Penedès, producing mostly cabernet-style wines. For a basic glass of red house wine, order *un tinto*. For quality wine, ask for *un crianza* (old), *un reserva* (older), or *un gran reserva* (oldest). Other popular wine drinks are *cava* (Spanish champagne), *tinto de varano* (wine with sweetened soda), and *jerez* (dry sherry, not the sweet dessert variety).

If you order a *caña* (small draft beer), you'll likely get one of the locally brewed lagers, Estrella Damm, Moritz, or various craft beers. A *clara con limón* is a small beer with lemonade. Nonalcoholic beer is quite popular (ask for *"una cerveza sin alcohol"*), as is nonalcoholic wine *(mosto)*. Bars often serve fresh-squeezed orange juice *(zumo de naranja natural)* and *horchata* (*orxata* in Catalan), a milky, nonalcoholic beverage made from *chufa* tubers.

Salud!

NEAR THE RAMBLAS—Handy, no-nonsense places within a few steps of the Ramblas; Metro: Liceu or Catalunya (see map, page 154)

1	**$ Taverna Basca Irati** Carrer del Cardenal Casanyes 17 tel. 933-023-084	Fun, user-friendly tapas bar, wide variety of Basque *pintxos* (daily 11:00-24:00)
2	**$ Restaurant Elisabets** Carrer d'Elisabets 2 tel. 933-175-826	Rough, popular local eatery, €11 lunch special, even cheaper *menú rapid* options 13:00-16:00, tapas, indifferent service (Mon-Sat 7:30-23:00, closed Sun and Aug)
3	**$ Café Granja Viader** Xuclà 4 tel. 933-183-486	Quaint, family-run, feminine-feeling place with baked goods, sandwiches, traditional breakfast, dairy-based sweets, *orxata* (Mon-Sat 9:00-13:00 & 17:00-21:00, closed Sun)
4	**$ La Boqueria Market** Ramblas #91	Picnic shopper's paradise for fresh produce, takeaway food, and cheap, colorful eateries (Mon-Sat 8:00-20:00, quiet after 16:00, closed Sun)
4	**$ Pinotxo Bar** Inside La Boqueria Market, on right-hand side tel. 933-171-731	Grab a stool for coffee, breakfast, tapas, and people-watching; fun-loving owner, don't overspend (Mon-Sat 8:00-20:00, closed Sun)
4	**$ Kiosko Universal** Inside La Boqueria Market, all the way to the left tel. 933-178-286	Line up for great-value, fresh-caught fish dishes amid market action, €8-12 *platos del día* (Mon-Sat 12:00-16:00, closed Sun)
5	**$$$ Casa Guinart** Inside La Boqueria Market, in far right corner tel. 933-178-887	Bohemian-chic with elegance and a great scene both inside and out, tables help you enjoy the market action (daily 10:00-24:00)
6	**$ Biocenter** Carrer del Pintor Fortuny 25 tel. 933-014-583	Vegetarian soup-and-salad restaurant, serious about food, €8-10 weekday lunch specials, €15 dinner (Mon-Sat 13:00-23:00, Sun 13:00-16:00)
7	**$$ Teresa Carles** Carrer Jovellanos 2 tel. 933-171-829	Classy and casual; vegetarian soups, salads, pastas, and risotto; €6-14 main dishes, €5 juices, breakfast available (daily 9:00-23:30)

BARRI GÒTIC—Atmospheric neighborhood with sit-down restaurants (listed first) and tapas bars; Metro: Jaume I, Catalunya, Liceu, or Drassanes (see map, page 154)

8	**$$ Café de l'Academia** Carrer dels Lledó 1 tel. 933-198-253	Delightful place on mellow square, local crowd, "refined cuisine," candlelit soft-jazz interior or outside (Mon-Fri 13:00-15:30 & 20:00-23:00, closed Sat-Sun)
9	**$$$ Els Quatre Gats** Carrer de Montsió 3 tel. 933-024-140	"The Four Cats" fed Picasso and now feeds tourists (go after 21:00), good food and service, not too overpriced, €18 lunch special Mon-Fri 13:00-16:00 (daily 10:00-24:00)
10	**$$ La Dolça Herminia** Carrer de les Magdalenes 27 tel. 933-170-676	Bright, modern Adilana chain restaurant, great-value Catalan/Mediterranean food, no reservations, notoriously busy (daily 13:00-15:45 & 20:30-23:30)
11	**$ Xaloc** Carrer de la Palla 13 tel. 933-011-990	Woody, modern place, gourmet tapas and home-style meals, fun energy, good service and prices, top-notch *jamón* (daily)
12	**$ Bar del Pi** Plaça de Sant Josep Oriol 1 tel. 933-022-123	Simple, hardworking bar for salads, sandwiches, and tapas; some outdoor tables on ultra-atmospheric little square (daily 9:00-23:00)
13	**$$ Restaurant Agut** Carrer d'En Gignàs 16 tel. 933-151-709	Around since 1924; modern, sophisticated, slightly bohemian, art-lined walls; tasty Catalan food, €14 lunch deal (Tue-Sat 13:30-16:00 & 20:30-23:30, Sun 13:30-16:00, closed Mon)
14	**$$ Les Quinze Nits** Plaça Reial 6 tel. 933-173-075	Bright, modern, and wildly popular (long lines, no reservations); artfully presented Spanish and Mediterranean cuisine at unbeatable prices, part of Andilana chain (daily 12:30-23:30, big dining room opens at 20:30)
15	**$$ La Crema Canela** Passatge de Madoz 6 tel. 933-182-744 www.grupandilana.com	Also part of Andilana chain, similar to Les Quinze Nits but feels cozier and takes reservations (daily 13:00-23:00, Fri-Sun until 23:30)

⑯	**$$ La Fonda** Carrer dels Escudellers 10 tel. 933-017-515	Another Andilana place, so expect good food, prices, ambience, and lines to get in (daily 13:00-23:30)
⑰	**$ Tapas Bars on Carrer de la Mercè** From the bottom of the Ramblas, hike east along Carrer de Josep Anselm Clavé	Street in unvarnished old Barcelona with greasy-spoon tapas bars; hop from bar to bar, enjoying cheap sardines, clams, and octopus (pulpo), all washed down with cider or €1 wine (most daily 11:00-23:00, liveliest 19:00-22:00)
⑱	**$$-$$$ Seafood Places in Barceloneta** From Metro: Barceloneta, head south along Passeig Joan de Borbó	Harborfront neighborhood facing the city has a number of classy if interchangeable seafood restaurants (try La Mar Salada at #58—open Wed-Mon for lunch and dinner, closed Tue)
IN EL BORN, NEAR THE PICASSO MUSEUM—Trendy, eclectic, classy bistros for foodies in small-lane neighborhood; Metro: Jaume I or Barceloneta (see map, page 154)		
⑲	**$ Bar del Pla** Carrer de Montcada 2 tel. 932-683-003	Local favorite, classic diner/bar for tapas and traditional dishes, same price at bar or table but bar has best scene (Mon-Sat 12:00-23:00, closed Sun)
⑳	**$$ El Senyor Parellada** Carrer de l'Argenteria 37 tel. 933-105-094	Former cloister, now white-tablecloth restaurant with smart, tourist-friendly staff; Catalan cuisine with modern twist (daily 13:00-15:45 & 20:30-23:30)
㉑	**$ Sagardi Euskal Taberna** Carrer de l'Argenteria 62 tel. 933-199-993	Lavish Basque tapas array, 20 percent more to sit outside, try Txakolí wine (daily 12:00-24:00)
㉑	**$$ Sagardi** Carrer de l'Argenteria 62 tel. 933-199-993	Mod but rustic restaurant for high-quality Basque steaks and grilled specialties, sizzling-grill ambience, reservations smart (daily 13:00-16:00 & 20:00-24:00)
㉒	**$$ El Xampanyet** Carrer de Montcada 22 tel. 933-197-003	Colorful, fun-loving, family-run tapas bar specializing in anchovies, tourists by day and locals by night, same price at bar or table (Tue-Sat 12:00-15:30 & 19:00-23:00, Sun 12:00-16:00, closed Mon)

㉓	**$ Taverna Tapeo** Carrer de Montcada 29 tel. 933-101-607	Classy alternative to the funky Xampanyet across the street; long bar and tiny tables serving near-gourmet tapas (Tue-Sun 12:00-16:00 & 19:00-24:00, closed Mon)
㉔	**$$ Bar Brutal** Carrer de la Barra de Ferro 1 tel. 932-954-797	Creative, fun-loving, and edgy bohemian-chic; mix of Spanish and Italian dishes with an emphasis on wines (Tue-Sat 13:00-24:00, closed Sun, also open Mon for dinner)
	THE EIXAMPLE—People-packed boulevards lined with upscale restaurants and tapas bars featuring breezy outdoor seating; Metro: Passeig de Gràcia, Provença, or Universitat (see map, page 156)	
㉕	**$$ La Rita** Near corner of Carrer de Pau at d'Aragó 279 tel. 934-872-376	Fresh and dressy little restaurant for Catalan cuisine, great-value fixed-price lunches (daily 13:00-15:45) and dinners (Sun-Thu 20:00-23:00, Fri-Sat 21:00-23:00), no reservations, arrive just before doors open
㉖	**$ La Bodegueta** Rambla de Catalunya 100 tel. 932-154-894	Atmospheric wine cellar for tapas, *anchoas* (anchovies), sandwiches *(flautas),* and vermouth; outside tables, €13 lunch special served Mon-Fri 13:00-16:00 (open Mon-Sat 7:00-24:00, Sun 18:30-24:00)
㉗	**$$ Restaurante la Palmera** Carrer d'Enric Granados 57 tel. 934-532-338 www.lapalmera.cat	Catalan, Mediterranean, and French cuisine, untouristy, great food and service, bottle-lined main room is best, reservations smart (Mon-Sat 13:00-15:45 & 20:00-23:15, closed Sun)
㉘	**$ La Flauta** Carrer d'Aribau 23 tel. 933-237-038	Fun, fresh, and modern; no-stress small-plate-and-sandwich menu, enthusiastic eaters, ground floor is best, €13 lunch deal (Mon-Sat 7:00-24:00, closed Sun)
㉙	**$$$ Cinc Sentits** Carrer d'Aribau 58 tel. 933-239-490 www.cincsentits.com	30-seat chic and snooty place for gourmets, fine service, beautifully presented avant-garde Catalan cuisine, €50-110 fixed-price extravaganzas, reservations required (Tue-Sat 13:30-15:00 & 20:30-22:00, closed Sun-Mon)

30	**$$ Mon Vinic** Carrer de la Diputació 249 tel. 932-726-187 www.monvinic.com	Sleek, trendy wine bar, evangelical about local wine culture, made-to-order Mediterranean dishes (Tue-Fri 13:30-23:00, Mon and Sat 19:00-23:00, closed Sun).
31	**$$ Tapas 24** Carrer de la Diputació 269 tel. 934-880-977	Fun local tapas bar, same price inside or out, happy energy, good yet pricey tapas from famous chef Carles Abellan (Mon-Sat 9:00-24:00, closed Sun)
32	**$ La Bodegueta Provença** Carrer de Provença 233 tel. 932-151-725	Lively tapas bar/café with multigenerational clientele, wow-inspiring half-kilo steak piled with Padrón peppers (daily 7:00-24:00)
33	**$$ Ciutat Comtal Cerveceria** Rambla de Catalunya 18 tel. 933-181-997	Classy tapas-only favorite brags about the best finger sandwiches *(montaditos)* and beers in Barcelona, eat inside or out (daily 8:00-24:00, packed 21:00-23:00)

Eating

Restaurants in the Old City

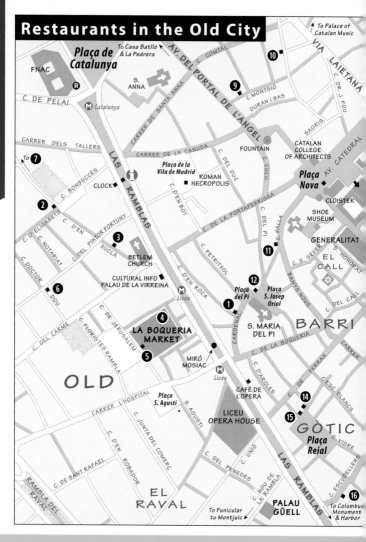

Plaça de Catalunya

To Palace of Catalan Music

FNAC

S. ANNA

R

C. DE PELAI

Catalunya

To Casa Batlló & La Pedrera

AV. DEL PORTAL DE L'ANGEL

C. COMTAL

10

VIA LAIETANA

C. DR. J. POU

9

C. MONTSIÓ

DURAN I BAS

SAGRIS

CATALAN COLLEGE OF ARCHITECTS

CARRER DE SANTA ANNA

CARRER DELS TALLERS

CARRER DE LA CANUDA

Plaça de la Vila de Madrid

ROMAN NECROPOLIS

FOUNTAIN

Plaça Nova

AV. CATEDRAL

To **7**

C. BONSUCCÉS

CLOCK

C. DEL DUC

C. DEN BOT

CLOISTER

SHOE MUSEUM

GENERALITAT

LAS RAMBLAS

2

C. D'ELISABETS

C. D'EN

C. DEL PINTOR FORTUNY

C. NOTARIAT

3

XUCLA

BETLEM CHURCH

CULTURAL INFO PALAU DE LA VIRREINA

C. DE LA PORTAFERRISSA

C. DEL PI

G. PALLA

C. PETRITXOL

C. S. SEVER

S. HONORAT

EL CALL

C. DOCTOR

C. DOU

6

C. DEN ROCA

Liceu

11

C. DE JERUSALEM

C. DE LA BOQUERIA

Plaça del Pi

12

Plaça S. Josep Oriol

BANYS NOUS

C. DEL CALL

1

4

LA BOQUERIA MARKET

5

MIRÓ MOSAIC

Liceu

S. MARIA DEL PI

BARRI

OLD

C. DEL CARME

G. FLORISTES RAMBLA

CARRER L'HOSPITAL

Plaça S. Agustí

S. AGUSTÍ

CAFÉ DE L'OPERA

C. D'AVINYO

C. DE FERRAN

C. D'ESC. BLANCS

14

CARRER

15

GÒTIC

EL RAVAL

C. D'EN ROBADOR

C. JUNTA DEL COMERÇ

C. DEL PENEDÈS

C. UNIÓ

LICEU OPERA HOUSE

Plaça Reial

C. VIDRE

RAMBLA DEL RAVAL

C. DE SANT RAFAEL

C. NOU DE LA RAMBLA

LAS RAMBLAS

C. ESCUDELLERS

16

PALAU GÜELL

To Funicular to Montjuïc

To Columbus Monument & Harbor

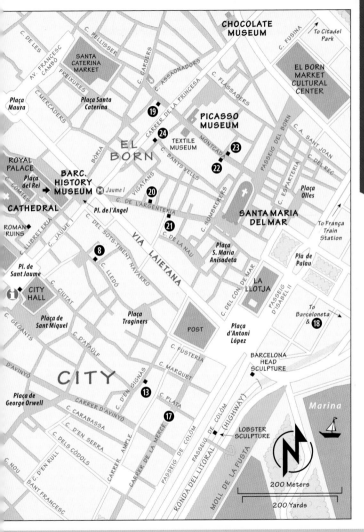

CHOCOLATE MUSEUM

To Citadel Park

C. FUSINA

C. FUSINA

EL BORN MARKET CULTURAL CENTER

C. DE LES

C. PELLISSER

C. CARDERS

SANTA CATERINA MARKET

AV. FRANCESC CAMBO

FREIXURES

C. ASSAONADORS

C. FLASSADERS

PASSEIG DEL BORN

C. A. SANT JOAN

C. DEL REC

Plaça Maura

C. MERCADERS

Plaça Santa Caterina

CARRER DE LA PRINCESA

PICASSO MUSEUM

19

24

TEXTILE MUSEUM

MONTCADA

23

22

C. ESPARTERIA

Plaça Olles

ROYAL PALACE

BORIA

EL BORN

C. BANYS VELLS

BARC. HISTORY MUSEUM

Plaça del Rei

VIGATANS

Jaume I

20

C. DE L'ARGENTERIA

C. SOMBRERERS

SANTA MARIA DEL MAR

C. COMTES

CATHEDRAL

Pl. de l'Angel

21

C. DE LA NAU

To França Train Station

ROMAN RUINS

C. LLIBRETERIA

C. JAUME I

VIA LAIETANA

Plaça S. Maria Anisadeta

Pla de Palau

Pl. de Sant Jaume

8

C. DEL SOTS-TINENT NAVARRO

C. DEL COM DE MAR

LA LLOTJA

CITY HALL

C. CIUTAT

C. LLEDÓ

PASSEIG D'ISABEL II

To Barceloneta & **18**

C. GEGANTS

Plaça de Sant Miquel

Plaça Traginers

POST

Plaça d'Antoni López

C. DATAULF

C. FUSTERIA

BARCELONA HEAD SCULPTURE

D'AVINYÓ

CITY

C. D'EN GIGNAS

C. MARQUET

Marina

Plaça de George Orwell

CARRER D'AVINYÓ

13

C. PLATA

PASSEIG DE COLÓM (HIGHWAY)

C. CARABASSA

17

LOBSTER SCULPTURE

N

C. D'EN SERRA

CARRER AMPLE

CARRER DE LA MERCÈ

PASSEIG DE COLÓM

C. DELS CODOLS

RONDA DEL LITORAL

MOLL DE LA FUSTA

C. NOU

C. D'EN RULL

SANT FRANCESC

200 Meters

200 Yards

Restaurants in the Eixample

To Sagrada Família

PALAU BARÓ DE QUADRAS

LA PEDRERA

M Diagonal

CARRER DE PROVENÇA

PASSEIG DE GRÀCIA

RAMBLA DE CATALUNYA

M Diagonal (To Sagrada Família)

CARRER DE MALLORCA

To Fontana & Lesseps & Casa Vicens

Provença

B M

PROVENÇA TRAIN STATION

R

C. DE VALÈNCIA

EIXAM

26

32

QUADRAT D'OR

PASSEIG DE GRÀCIA TRAIN STATION

25

R

Passeig de Gràcia

CASA BATLLÓ

FUNDACIÓ TÀPIES

CASA AMATLLER

CASA LLEÓ MORERA

BLOCK OF DISCORD

RAMBLA DE CATALUNYA

CARRER DE BALMES

CARRER D'ENRIC GRANADOS

27

CARRER DE VALÈNCIA

CARRER D'ARIBAU

Plaça del Doctor Letamendi

CARRER DEL CONSELL DE CENT

30

29

CARRER DE LA DIPUTACIÓ

28

GRAN VIA

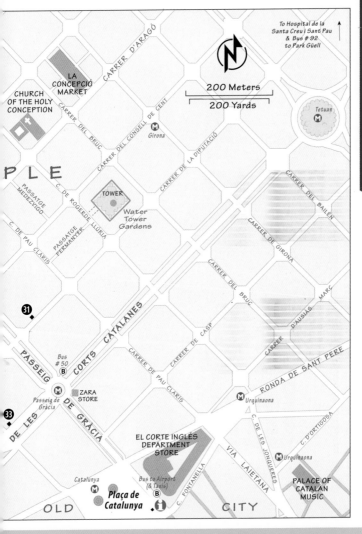

To Hospital de la
Santa Creu i Sant Pau
& Bus #92
to Park Güell

200 Meters

200 Yards

CARRER D'ARAGÓ

LA CONCEPCIÓ MARKET

CHURCH OF THE HOLY CONCEPTION

CARRER DEL BRUC

CARRER DEL CONSELL DE CENT

Girona Ⓜ

CARRER DE LA DIPUTACIÓ

P L E

CARRER DEL BAILÉN

CARRER DE GIRONA

Tetuan Ⓜ

PASSATGE MEDEZVGO

C. DE ROGER DE LLÚRIA

TOWER

Water Tower Gardens

PASSATGE PERMANYER

C. DE PAU CLARIS

CARRER DEL BRUC

CARRER D'AUSIÀS MARC

CARRER DE CASP

❸ꝑ

Ⓑ Bus #50

CORTS CATALANES

CARRER DE PAU CLARIS

RONDA DE SANT PERE

Ⓜ Urquinaona

PASSEIG DE GRÀCIA

Ⓜ Passeig de Gràcia

ZARA STORE

❸ꝑ

DE LES

EL CORTE INGLÉS DEPARTMENT STORE

C. DE LES JONQUERES

Ⓜ Urquinaona

C. D'ORTIGOSA

Catalunya Ⓜ

Ⓑ Bus to Airport (& Taxis)

C. FONTANELLA

VIA LAIETANA

PALACE OF CATALAN MUSIC

Plaça de Catalunya

OLD

CITY

Practicalities

Planning 160	Theft and Emergencies. 171
Money. 161	Activities 172
Arrival in Barcelona 162	Resources
Helpful Hints 163	from Rick Steves 178
Getting Around Barcelona . . 165	Spanish Survival Phrases . . . 179
Communicating. 168	Catalan Survival Phrases . . . 181
Sightseeing Tips 170	

Helpful Websites

Spanish Tourist Information: www.spain.info
Barcelona Tourist Information: www.barcelonaturisme.cat
Other Helpful Barcelona Websites: www.barcelonaplanning.com,
www.guiadelocio.com/barcelona, and www.butxaca.com
Cheap Flights: www.kayak.com (for international flights), www.
skyscanner.com (for flights within Europe)
Train Schedules: www.renfe.com (Spanish national railway), www.
bahn.com (best site for European rail)
General Travel Tips: www.ricksteves.com (helpful info on train travel,
rail passes, car rental, using your mobile device, travel insurance, packing lists, and much more—plus updates to this book)

PLANNING

When to Go

Sea breezes off the Mediterranean make Barcelona pleasant for much
of the year. Late spring and early fall offer the best combination of good
weather (in the low 70s), light crowds, long days, and plenty of tourist and
cultural activities. July and August bring hot, humid weather (in the low
80s) and the biggest crowds, and some shops and restaurants close down
in August. Winter temperatures are mild (mid-50s). Expect some rain one
day a week throughout the year. Barcelona's many festivals can bring especially big crowds and fill up hotels.

Before You Go

Make sure your passport is up to date (to renew, see www.travel.state.
gov). Call your debit- and credit-card companies about your plans. Book
hotel rooms and make reservations for key sights, especially for travel during peak season or holiday weekends. Consider buying travel insurance
(see www.ricksteves.com/insurance). If traveling beyond Barcelona, re-
search transit schedules (trains, buses) and car rentals. Barcelona makes
a good first or last stop on a Spain trip: It's easy to fly into Barcelona, then
travel to Madrid on a 2.5-hour AVE train (www.renfe.com) or cheap flight,
such as on Vueling Air (www.vueling.com).

Tipping

Spaniards rarely tip, so tipping in Spain isn't as automatic and generous as it is in the US. If you order at a counter—such as sampling tapas at a bar—there's no need to tip (you can throw in a few small coins if you wish). At Spanish restaurants that have table service, a service charge is generally included in the bill (*servei inclós* in Catalan, or *servicio incluido* in Spanish). Spaniards don't tip beyond this, but if the service is exceptional, you can round up by as much as 5 percent. To tip a taxi driver, round up to the nearest euro (for a €5.50 fare, give €6), or up to 10 percent for longer rides. In general, if someone in the service industry does a super job for you, a small tip of a euro or two is appropriate...but not required.

MONEY

Spain uses the euro currency: 1 euro (€) = about $1.10. To convert prices in euros to dollars, add about 10 percent: €20 = about $22, €50 = about $55. (Check www.oanda.com for the latest exchange rates.)

Withdraw money from an ATM (*cajero automático* in Spanish, *caixer automàtic* in Catalan) using a debit card, just like at home. Visa and MasterCard are commonly used throughout Europe. Before departing, call your bank and credit-card company: Confirm that your card will work overseas, ask about international transaction fees, and alert them that you'll be making withdrawals in Europe. Many travelers bring a second (or third) debit/credit card as a backup. Cash is always good to have on hand, so withdraw large amounts (€250-300) from the ATM.

American credit cards—even new ones with a chip—may not work in some payment machines (e.g., ticket kiosks) geared for European-style chip-and-PIN cards. Be prepared to pay with cash, try entering your card's PIN, or find a nearby cashier.

To keep your valuables safe, wear a money belt. But if you do lose your credit or debit card, report the loss immediately with a phone call: Visa (tel. 303/967-1096), MasterCard (tel. 636/722-7111), and American Express (tel. 336/393-1111).

ARRIVAL IN BARCELONA

I don't recommend driving in Barcelona. Even parking a car here is expensive. If you're renting a car for a Spain trip, it's better to do it in Madrid, and connect to Barcelona by train or air.

El Prat de Llobregat Airport

Barcelona's airport has two large terminals, linked by shuttle buses. Most airlines use Terminal 1. Both terminals have the necessary services—TI, post office, pharmacy, a left-luggage office, eateries, and ATMs. Use the bank-affiliated ATMs in the main arrivals hall (airport code: BCN, tel. 913-211-000, www.aena-aeropuertos.es). To get between the airport and downtown Barcelona (8 miles southwest of town), you have three options:

Taxi: A taxi for the 30-minute trip into town costs about €35 (including €3.10 airport supplement).

Bus: The Aerobus leaves from immediately outside the arrivals lobby of both terminals (bus #A1 for Terminal 1 and #A2 for Terminal 2). In about 30 minutes you arrive downtown, with stops at Plaça d'Espanya and Plaça de Catalunya (departs every 5 minutes, from airport 6:00-1:00 in the morning, from downtown 5:30-24:15, €5.90 one-way, €10.20 round-trip, buy ticket from machine or driver, tel. 934-156-020, www.aerobusbcn.com).

Train: The RENFE train (on the "R2 Sud" Rodalies line) leaves from Terminal 2 only, heading to Sants Station, Passeig de Gràcia Station (near Plaça de Catalunya), and França Station (10-minute walk from Terminal 2 to the station—follow signs, departs 2/hour, €4.10 or covered by T10 Card).

Sants Train Station

Barcelona has several train stations, but virtually all trains (including the AVE from Madrid) end up at Sants, located west of the Old City. It's vast but manageable, with a TI, ATMs, shops, eateries, a classy Sala Club lounge for travelers with first-class reservations, and luggage storage (€5/day, near tracks 13-14). If you need train tickets (it's smart to reserve a day ahead in Spain), you can wait in line at the station, or use helpful travel agencies in many El Corte Inglés department stores. It's also possible by phone (tel. 902-240-202), at www.renfe.com (may not accept US credit cards), or at www.raileurope.com (fee).

To get downtown, take the Metro. The L3 (green) and L5 (blue) lines link to a number of useful points in town. Alternatively, you can take any Rodalies suburban train from track 8 (R1, R3, or R4) to Plaça de Catalunya.

Cruise Ship Ports

Most American cruise lines put in at Moll Adossat/Muelle Adosado, beneath Montjuïc, two miles from the bottom of the Ramblas. For the trip into town, taxis are always waiting—it's about €15 to the Ramblas or Plaça de Catalunya. Or you can take the #T3 shuttle bus to the bottom of the Ramblas (also called Bus Port; follow *Public Bus* signs, €3.50 round-trip, tel. 932-986-000).

HELPFUL HINTS

Tourist Information (TI): Barcelona's TI has several branches (central tel. 932-853-834, www.barcelonaturisme.cat). The main TI is beneath Plaça de Catalunya (daily 8:30-20:30, entrance just across from El Corte Inglés department store—look for red sign and take stairs down, tel. 932-853-832). The privately run Ruta de Modernisme desk is located here. Other convenient branches in the Old City are near the top of the Ramblas at #115 (mobile 618-783-479), on Plaça de Sant Jaume, and at the Columbus Monument. In the Eixample neighborhood, the Catalunya TI gives tips on Barcelona and the entire region (Passeig de Gràcia 107, tel. 932-388-091, www.catalunya.com). There are TIs at the airport and at Sants train station. Besides these major TIs, helpful kiosks (and young, red-jacketed helpers) often spring up in touristy locales.

At any TI, pick up the free city map (although the free El Corte Inglés map provided by most hotels is better), the small Metro map, and various free periodicals with sightseeing tips, shopping, events, and restaurants.

TIs are handy places to buy tickets for the hop-on hop-off Tourist Bus or for the TI-run walking tours (both described later). Most TIs also provide a room-booking service.

Hurdling the Language Barrier: Many Barcelonans prefer the Catalan language, though everyone also speaks Spanish *(castellano)*. Signs almost always list both. Most people in the tourist industry—and virtually all young people—speak at least a little English. Get a start learning a little Catalan and Spanish with the survival phrases on ✪ pages 179-182.

Time Zones: Spain's time zone is generally six/nine hours ahead of the East/West Coasts of the US.

Business Hours: Many businesses respect the afternoon siesta, when locals break for their main meal and get out of the afternoon heat. Shops are generally open Monday through Saturday 10:00-13:00 and 16:00-20:00, though some shops may not be open Saturday evenings. Tourist-friendly shops are often open on Sunday. Banking hours are generally Monday through Friday 9:00-14:00.

Holidays: Many sights and banks close down on national holidays. Barcelona celebrates more local festivals than most places. Verify dates at www.barcelonaturisme.cat, or check www.ricksteves.com/festivals.

Watt's Up? Europe's electrical system is 220 volts, instead of North America's 110 volts. Most newer electronics (including hair dryers, laptops, and battery chargers) convert automatically, so you won't need a converter—but you will need a adapter plug with two round prongs, sold inexpensively at US and Canadian travel stores.

Numbers and Stumblers: What Americans call the second floor of a building is the first floor in Europe. Europeans write dates as day/month/year, so Christmas 2016 is 25/12/16. Commas are decimal points and vice versa—a dollar and a half is 1,50, and there are 5.280 feet in a mile. Spain uses the metric system: A kilogram is 2.2 pounds; a liter is about a quart; and a kilometer is six-tenths of a mile. Temperature is measured in Celsius. 0°C = 32°F. To convert Celsius to Fahrenheit, double the number and add 30.

Laundry: Several self-service launderettes (€8/load) are located around the Old City. LavaXpres is near Plaça de Catalunya at Passatge d'Elisabets 3 (daily 8:00-22:00). Wash 'n Dry is a block west of the Ramblas, near Palau Güell, at Carrer Nou de la Rambla 19 (daily 9:00-23:00).

Services: Public WCs are scarce. Use them when you can, in any café or museum you patronize.

GETTING AROUND BARCELONA

Barcelona is big enough that, at some point, you will need to take public transportation. The Old City (Ramblas and Barri Gòtic) is great for walking. But taxis and the Metro make the rest of the city easily accessible.

By Metro

The city's Metro (www.tmb.cat) is among Europe's best, connecting just about every place you'll visit. A single-ride ticket (€2.15) covers 1.25 hours of unlimited use (including transfers) on the Metro, bus, and several sub-urban train lines. The T10 Card is a great deal—€9.95 gives you 10 rides, cutting the per-ride cost more than in half. Travel companions can share a T10 Card. Multiday passes are also available (2 days-€14, 5 days-€32). Machines at the Metro entrance have English instructions and sell all types of tickets (most accept credit/debit cards as well as cash).

The Metro works like most any transit system. Find signs for your line number—for example, the "L3." Then find the L3 train headed the direction you're going (e.g., "L3 - Trinitata Nova"). Insert your ticket into the turnstile (with the arrow pointing in), then reclaim it and hold on to it until you exit. Keep your bags close by and beware pickpockets.

The most useful line for tourists is the L3 (green). Handy stops include (in order):

Sants Estació—Main train station

Espanya—Plaça d'Espanya, at the bottom of Montjuïc

Paral-lel—Funicular to the top of Montjuïc

Drassanes—Bottom of the Ramblas, near Maritime Museum and Maremagnum mall

Liceu—Middle of the Ramblas, near the heart of the Barri Gòtic and cathedral

Plaça de Catalunya—Top of the Ramblas and main square with TI, airport bus, and lots of transportation connections

Passeig de Gràcia—Eixample, Block of Discord, transfer to the L2 (purple) line to Sagrada Família and L4 (yellow) line (described below)

Diagonal—La Pedrera

The L4 (yellow) line is also useful, with stops at Joanic (bus #116 to Park Güell), Jaume I (near Plaça de Sant Jaume and Picasso Museum), and Barceloneta (the harbor).

Barcelona's Public Transportation

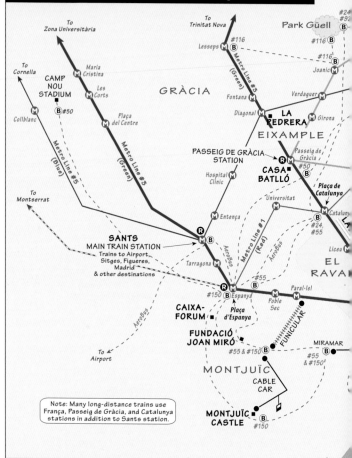

To Zona Universitària

To Cornella

To Trinitat Nova

Park Güell

#24
#92

#116 ⒷⓃ

Lesseps Ⓑ#116

#116 Ⓑ

Joanic Ⓜ

CAMP NOU STADIUM

Ⓑ#50

Maria Cristina Ⓜ

Les Corts Ⓜ

Plaça del Centre Ⓜ

Collblanc

GRÀCIA

Metro Line #3 (Green)

Fontana Ⓜ

Verdaguer Ⓜ

Diagonal Ⓜ ■ LA PEDRERA

Girona Ⓜ

EIXAMPLE

Passeig de Gràcia Ⓜ

#50

PASSEIG DE GRÀCIA STATION ⒷⓇ

CASA BATLLÓ

Hospital Clínic Ⓜ

Plaça de Catalunya

To Montserrat

Metro Line #5 (Blue)

Universitat Ⓜ

Entença Ⓜ

Catalunya Ⓜ

LA

#24, #55

SANTS MAIN TRAIN STATION
Trains to Airport, Sitges, Figueres, Madrid & other destinations

Ⓡ Ⓜ Ⓑ

Tarragona Ⓜ

AeroBus

Metro Line #1 (Red)

AeroBus

Liceu Ⓜ

EL RAVA

#55

ⒷⓇⓂ #150 Ⓑ Espanya

Poble Sec Ⓜ

Paral·lel Ⓜ

CAIXA-FORUM ■

Plaça d'Espanya

AeroBus

To Airport

FUNICULAR

FUNDACIÓ JOAN MIRÓ ■

#55 & #150 Ⓑ

MIRAMAR ●

#55 & #150

MONTJUÏC

CABLE CAR

MONTJUÏC CASTLE Ⓑ

#150

Note: Many long-distance trains use França, Passeig de Gràcia, and Catalunya stations in addition to Sants station.

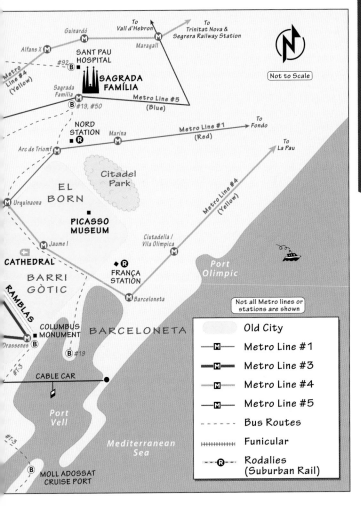

To Vall d'Hebron

To Trinitat Nova & Segrera Railway Station

Guinardó

Maragall

Alfons X Ⓜ

SANT PAU HOSPITAL

Ⓑ #92

Metro Line #4 (Yellow)

Sagrada Família

SAGRADA FAMÍLIA

Ⓑ #19, #50

Metro Line #5 (Blue)

N

Not to Scale

NORD STATION Ⓡ

Marina Ⓜ

Metro Line #1 (Red)

To Fondo

Arc de Triomf Ⓜ

To La Pau

CITADEL PARK

Metro Line #4 (Yellow)

EL BORN

Urquinaona Ⓜ

PICASSO MUSEUM

Jaume I Ⓜ

Ciutadella / Vila Olímpica Ⓜ

Port Olímpic

CATHEDRAL

BARRI GÒTIC

FRANÇA STATION Ⓡ

RAMBLAS

Barceloneta Ⓜ

Not all Metro lines or stations are shown

COLUMBUS MONUMENT

BARCELONETA

Drassanes Ⓑ

Ⓑ #19

#T-3

Old City

Ⓜ Metro Line #1

Ⓜ Metro Line #3

Ⓜ Metro Line #4

Ⓜ Metro Line #5

Bus Routes

Funicular

Ⓡ Rodalies (Suburban Rail)

CABLE CAR

Port Vell

Mediterranean Sea

#T-3

Ⓑ MOLL ADOSSAT CRUISE PORT

By Taxi

Barcelona is one of Europe's best taxi towns. Taxis are plentiful, rates are clearly posted in every cab, and prices are reasonable. Flag down any cab with its green rooftop light on. By day (7:00-21:00) they charge *Tarif 2* (€1/kilometer plus €2.10 drop charge). You'll pay more after hours *(Tarif 1),* for luggage, and surcharges to/from the train station or airport. A typical ride from Sants Station to the Ramblas costs about €10.

By Bus

Given the excellent Metro service, it's unlikely you'll spend much time on local buses (also €2.15, covered by T10 Card, insert ticket in machine behind driver). However, buses can be handy for visiting Park Güell, Montjuïc, and the beach. More useful are the **hop-on hop-off tour buses** (✪ see page 176).

By Bike

Barcelona's traffic is probably too stressful to use a bike for most point-to-point travel. But joy-riding is wonderful in the Eixample, in Citadel Park, and along the Barceloneta beach. If you want to try biking but are intimidated by the traffic, consider taking a bike tour (described later, under "Activities").

Several places rent bikes for around €5 per hour (cheaper for longer rentals, may require a deposit). In the Old City, there's the helpful Barcelona by Bicycle, near the Church of Santa Maria del Mar at Carrer de l'Esparteria 3 (tel. 932-682-105). Barcelona Rent-A-Bike is four blocks from the Barceloneta Metro stop at Passeig de Joan de Borbó 35 (tel. 933-212-790). On the Barceloneta beach, there's Biciclot, at Passeig Maritime 33 (tel. 932-219-778). In Citadel Park there are several rental places. Elsewhere, you'll see racks of government-subsidized "Bicing" borrow-a-bikes—but these are only for locals, not tourists.

COMMUNICATING

The easiest (if not cheapest) way to stay connected while on the road—planning your sightseeing, contacting hotels, and staying in touch—is to bring your own mobile device (phone, smartphone, tablet, or laptop) and keep your home carrier. But you can also do fine bringing no device at

Useful Contacts

Police: Tel. 091 (nationwide) or 092 (local)
Ambulance or any Emergency: Tel. 112
US Consulate: Tel. 932-802-227, after-hours emergency tel. 915-872-200, Paseo Reina Elisenda de Montcada 23, http://barcelona.usconsulate.gov
Canadian Consulate: Tel. 932-703-614, after-hours emergency tel. in Ottawa—call collect 613-996-8885, Plaça de Catalunya 9, www.spain.gc.ca
Collect Calls to the US: Dial 900-99-0011 (press zero or stay on the line for an English-speaking operator)
Directory Assistance: Tel. 11811 (€0.40/minute) or 11818 (€0.55/call from private numbers, free from phone booths)

all, relying only on your hotel's guest computer, Internet cafés, and public phones. Read on for more details and budget alternatives. For more on all of these options, see www.ricksteves.com/phoning.

Using the Internet: Traveling with a mobile device gives you on-the-go access to the Internet and travel-oriented apps. You can make free or cheap phone calls using Skype, Google+ Hangouts, or FaceTime. CityMaps2Go has free street maps that can be used offline.

To avoid sky-high fees for data roaming (about $20 to download one megabyte of data), disable data roaming entirely, and only go online when you have Wi-Fi (e.g., at your hotel or at a public hot spot). Or you could sign up for an international data plan for the duration of your trip to reduce the cost.

Almost all hotels offer some form of free or cheap Internet access—either a shared computer in the lobby or Wi-Fi. Otherwise, your hotelier can point you to the nearest Internet café. You'll also find Wi-Fi hotspots at many cafés. The free city network, Barcelona Wi-Fi, has hundreds of hotspots around town; just look for the blue diamond-shaped sign with a big "W" (for details, see www.bcn.cat/barcelonawifi).

Making Phone Calls: Most US mobile phones work in Europe. Expect to pay around $1.50 a minute for phone calls and 50 cents per text message (less if you sign up for an international calling plan with your service provider). If you plan to make a lot of calls, consider outfitting your phone with a European SIM card—that is, temporarily sign up with a European carrier. (For more on how SIM cards work, see www.ricksteves.com/phoning).

It's easy to buy a phone in Europe, which costs more up front but is cheaper by the call. You'll find mobile-phone stores selling cheap phones (for $40 or less) and SIM cards at the airport and train stations, and throughout Spain.

Dialing Tips: Always start with the **international access code**— 011 if calling from the US or Canada, 00 from anywhere in Europe. If you're dialing from a mobile phone, simply insert a + instead (by holding the 0 key). To call **from the US to Spain**, dial 011 (US access code), 34 (Spain's country code), and the local number. To call from **any European country to the US,** dial 00 (Europe's access code), 1 (US country code), then the area code and local number. To call **within Spain,** just dial the local number (Spain doesn't use area codes). If you're calling from Europe using your US mobile phone, dial as if you're calling from the US.

Phoning Inexpensively: Here's a budget alternative if you don't carry a mobile phone: Buy an international phone card (€5). This gives you pennies-per-minute rates on international calls, decent rates for calls within Spain, and can even be used from your hotel phone or a European mobile phone. Buy cards at newsstands, electronics stores, and Internet cafés. Calling from your hotel room without a phone card can be a rip-off—ask your hotelier about their rates before you dial.

SIGHTSEEING TIPS

Make reservations to avoid lines. You'll need reservations if you want to visit Barcelona's Casa Lleó Morera (✪ see page 121) or the Palace of Catalan Music (✪ see page 117). Avoid entrance lines of an hour or more by reserving in advance for the Picasso Museum (✪ see page 64), Sagrada Família (✪ page 94), Casa Batlló (✪ page 120), La Pedrera (✪ see page 122), Palau Güell (✪ see page 110), and Park Güell's Monumental Zone (✪ see page 125). Another line-skipping option is the...

Articket BCN Sightseeing Pass: For €30, you get admission to six art museums—and you can skip the ticket-buying lines. It includes the recommended Picasso Museum, Catalan Art Museum, and Fundació Joan

Miró. If you visit three or more museums, it's worth it. The pass is sold at participating museums and some TIs (www.articketbcn.org). I'd skip the Barcelona Card, which covers public transportation and a few minor sights.

Hours: Since opening hours can change year-to-year, it's always wise to get the most up-to-date at the TI or www.barcelonaturisme.com. Be aware that many top sights are closed on Monday—making them especially crowded on Tuesday and Sunday.

Typical Rules: Some sights have metal detectors or conduct bag searches that will slow your entry. Some don't allow large bags and may not allow you to bring liquids (water bottles) in. Photos and videos are normally allowed, but flashes or tripods usually are not.

Discounts: Many sights offer discounts for youths (up to age 18), students (with proper identification cards, www.isic.org), families, seniors (loosely defined as retirees or those willing to call themselves seniors), and groups of 10 or more. Always ask. Some discounts are only for EU citizens.

Pace Yourself: Schedule cool breaks into your sightseeing where you can sit and refresh with a drink or snack.

THEFT AND EMERGENCIES

Theft: While violent crime is rare, thieves (mainly pickpockets) thrive in crowds. Be alert to the possibility of theft, especially when you're absorbed in the wonder and newness of Barcelona. You're more likely to be pickpocketed in Barcelona—especially along the Ramblas—than just about anywhere else in Europe.

Here are some common scams: a too-friendly local who engages you in conversation while he picks your pocket; thieves posing as lost tourists who ask for your help; street gamblers playing shell games; and groups of women aggressively "selling carnations," while actually rifling your pocket. If you encounter any commotion or distraction on the Ramblas, put your hands in your pockets before someone else does.

Some neighborhoods feel seedy and can be unsafe after dark. I'd avoid the lower part of the Barri Gòtic south and east of Plaça Reial (though the strip near the Carrer de la Mercè tapas bars is better). Don't venture too deep into the Raval (just west of the Ramblas). One block can separate a comfy tourist zone from junkies and prostitutes.

I keep my valuables—passport, credit cards, crucial documents, and large amounts of cash—in a money belt that I tuck under my clothes. Dial 091 or 092 for police help. To replace a passport, contact an embassy or consulate (for contact info, ✪ see page 169). File a police report without delay; it's required to submit an insurance claim for lost or stolen rail passes or travel gear, and can help with replacing your passport or credit and debit cards. For more information, see www.ricksteves.com/help.

Medical Help: Dial 112 for any emergency (medical or otherwise). If you get sick, do as the Spanish do and go to a pharmacy, where qualified technicians routinely diagnose and prescribe. There's a 24-hour pharmacy across from La Boqueria Market at Ramblas #98, and another near La Pedrera. Or ask at your hotel for help—they'll know the nearest medical and emergency services.

ACTIVITIES

Shopping

Whatever your taste or budget, Barcelona is a fantastic shopping city. The streets of the Barri Gòtic and El Born are bursting with characteristic hole-in-the-wall shops, while the Eixample is the upscale "uptown" shopping district. Near Plaça de Catalunya, Avinguda del Portal de l'Angel has a staggering array of department and chain stores.

Souvenir Items: In this artistic city, consider picking up Picasso prints, Dalí posters, Miró magnets, and books about Gaudí. Museum gift shops (Picasso Museum and La Pedrera) are open to the public and a bonanza for art and design lovers. Home-decor shops have Euro-style housewares unavailable back home and Modernista-flavored glassware. Decorative tile and pottery (popularized by Modernist architects) and Modernista jewelry are easy to pack. Foodies might bring back olive oil, wine, spices (such as saffron or sea salts), cheese, or the local nougat treat, *torró*. (See below for US customs rules on foods.) An *espardenya*—or *alpargata* in Spanish—is a soft-canvas, rope-soled shoe (known in the US as an espadrille) that originated as humble peasant footwear. For a souvenir of Catalan culture, consider a Catalan flag (gold and red stripes), or a jersey or scarf from the wildly popular Barça soccer team.

Sizes: European clothing sizes are different from the US. For example, a woman's size 10 dress (US) is a European size 40, and a size 8 shoe (US) is a European size 38-39.

Getting a VAT Refund: If you spend more than €90 on goods at a single store, you may be eligible to get a refund of the 21 percent Value-Added Tax (VAT). You'll need to ask the merchant to fill out the necessary refund document, then process your refund through a service such as Global Blue or Premier Tax Free, with offices at major airports. For more details, see www.ricksteves.com/vat.

Customs for American Shoppers: You are allowed to take home $800 worth of items per person duty-free, once every 30 days. You can also bring in duty-free a liter of alcohol. As for food, you can take home many processed and packaged foods (e.g., vacuum-packed cheeses, chocolate, mustard). Fresh produce and most meats are not allowed, but some canned items are okay. Any liquid-containing foods must be packed (carefully) in checked luggage. To check customs rules and duty rates, visit http://help.cbp.gov.

Shopping Neighborhoods

Barri Gòtic: Stroll from the cathedral to the Ramblas, through interesting streets lined with little local shops. Avoid the midafternoon siesta and Sundays, when many shops are closed.

Face the cathedral, turn 90 degrees right, and exit Plaça Nova (just to the left of the Bilbao Berria "BB" restaurant) on the tight lane called Carrer de la Palla. This street has a half-dozen antique shops crammed with mothballed treasures. Mixed in are a few art galleries, offbeat shops, and a motorcycle museum. When you reach the fork in the road (where the inviting Caelum café is), take the right fork. You'll pass by Oro Líquido ("Liquid Gold"), which sells high-quality olive oils.

You'll soon reach the Church of Santa Maria del Pi ringed by a charming, café-lined square. Skirt around the right side of the church to find Josep Roca, a genteel gentleman's shop.

From Josep Roca, head up narrow Carrer de Petritxol ("peht-ree-CHUHL"). It's a fun combination of art galleries, fancy jewelry shops, and simple places for hot chocolate and churros (check out Granja La Pallaresa, just after #11).

You'll dead-end onto Carrer de la Portaferrissa, with its international teen clothing stores. From here, you can turn left to reach the Ramblas, or turn right to return to the cathedral.

Eixample: This ritzy "uptown" district is home to some of the city's top-end shops. From Plaça de Catalunya, head north up Passeig de Gràcia. You'll pass by lower-end international stores (Zara, Mango, Camper) at the lower end of the street, to top-end brands at the top (Gucci, Luis Vuitton, Escada, Chanel). Near La Pedrera, check out Vinçon (Passeig de Gràcia 96), a sprawling Euro-housewares store that feels like a trendy Spanish Ikea. Detour one block west to Rambla de Catalunya, with more local (but still expensive) options.

El Born: For a nice route through this boutique-speckled neighborhood, ✪ see the El Born Walk in the Sights chapter (page 114).

Placa de Catalunya and Avinguda Portal de l'Angel: Barcelona natives do most of their shopping at big department stores. Get a sense of contemporary Spanish fashion by strolling down the street that runs south from Placa de Catalunya. El Corte Inglés is the Spanish answer to one-stop shopping—everything from clothes to furniture to electronics, bonsai trees, a travel agency, groceries, and haircuts. The Spanish chain Zara and Barcelona-based Mango focus on clothes. Women's Secret is the Spanish answer to Victoria's Secret, Pull and Bear is the Spanish Gap, and Camper does shoes. Also along the street are numerous international chains, from the teen-oriented French chain Pimkie to Italy's Intimissimi, to conglomerates like H&M, Esprit, and Benetton.

Nightlife

For their evening entertainment, Barcelonans stroll the streets, greeting neighbors, popping into a bar for drinks and tapas, nursing a cocktail on a floodlit square, or enjoying a late meal. Dinnertime is around 22:00, and even families with children can be out well after midnight. The liveliest neighborhoods are the funky El Born, the ritzy Eixample, the touristy Barri Gòtic, and the always-crowded Ramblas.

In addition, Barcelona always has a vast array of cultural events. The TI hands out the free monthly English-language *Time Out BCN Guide.* Another good source of information is the Palau de la Virreina ticket office (Ramblas 99, tel. 933-161-000). Or check http://barcelonacultura.bcn.cat.

You can buy tickets directly from the venue, from box offices at El Corte Inglés or the FNAC store (both on Plaça de Catalunya), from Palau de la Virreina, or at www.ticketmaster.es or www.telentrada.com.

Live Music: The Palace of Catalan Music (Palau de la Música Catalana), with one of the finest Modernista interiors in town (✪ see listing on page 117), offers everything from symphonic to Catalan folk songs to chamber music to flamenco (€20-50 tickets, Carrer Palau de la Música 4, Metro: Urquinaona, tel. 902-442-882, www.palaumusica.cat).

The Liceu Opera House (Gran Teatre del Liceu), right in the heart of the Ramblas, is a sumptuous venue for opera, dance, and concerts (tickets from €10, La Rambla 51, box office just around the corner at Carrer Sant Pau 1, Metro: Liceu, tel. 934-859-913, www.liceubarcelona.cat).

Other classy venues occasionally hosting concerts are La Pedrera (www.lapedrera.com), Fundació Joan Miró (www.fundaciomiro-bcn. org), and CaixaForum (http://obrasocial.lacaixa.es—choose "CaixaForum Barcelona").

"Masters of Guitar" concerts are offered nearly nightly at 21:00 in the Barri Gòtic's Church of Santa Maria del Pi (€23 at the door, Plaça del Pi 7, tel. 647-514-513, www.maestrosdelaguitarra.com).

Though flamenco music is not typical of Barcelona (it's from Andalucía), you'll find entertaining concerts nightly at Tarantos, on Plaça Reial (at #17, tel. 933-191-789, www.masimas.com/en/tarantos).

La Pedrera (Casa Milà) hosts the "Summer Nights at La Pedrera" concerts (mostly jazz) on its fanciful floodlit rooftop, weekends from June to September (book ahead at tel. 902-101-212 or www.lapedrera.com).

Hotel Casa Fuster, a Modernista landmark, has jazz every Thursday at 21:00 (€19 "membership" required, reservations recommended, north of Avinguda Diagonal at Passeig de Gràcia 132, tel. 932-553-006, www. cafevienesjazzclub.blogspot.com).

Jamboree, right on Plaça Reial, has jazz nightly at 20:00 and 22:00 in its cellar (€5-20, Plaça Reial 17, tel. 933-191-789, www.masimas.com/en/jamboree).

Evening Sightseeing: For a list of sights open in the evening (19:30 or later), ✪ see page 11. The hop-on, hop-off Tourist Bus runs until 20:00 daily in summer. The illuminated Magic Fountains on Montjuïc also make a good finale for your day.

After-Hours Neighborhoods

Join bar-hopping Barcelonans for tapas, drinks, and dancing into the wee hours. The weekend ritual (Thu-Sat) might go something like this: evening tapas; dinner around 22:00; a music club for cocktails and DJ music from midnight; then, at about 2:00 or 3:00 in the morning, hit the discos until dawn. The following neighborhoods party late, but they're also lively for tapas and drinks in the early evening.

El Born: Passeig del Born, a broad park-like strip stretching from the Church of Santa Maria del Mar, is lined with inviting bars and nightspots. Wander the side streets for more options. Miramelindo is a local favorite for mojitos (Passeig del Born 15). La Vinya del Senyor is mellower, for tapas and wine on the square in front of the church.

Plaça Reial (in the Barri Gòtic): A block off the Ramblas, this palm-tree-graced square bustles with trendy eateries charging inflated prices for pleasant outdoor tables—perfect for nursing a drink (try the Ocaña Bar at #13). Or buy a €1 beer from a convenience store and lean against a palm tree. Plaça Reial is also home to the Tarantos flamenco bar and Jamboree jazz club (both described earlier), plus the hip Sidecar Factory Club (at #7, often live music, www.sidecarfactoryclub.com) and the hidden, mellow, pipe-happy Barcelona Pipa Club (at #3—find and ring the doorbell to get inside, this member's club opens to the public around 22:00, www.bpipaclub.com).

Carrer de la Mercè: This Barri Gòtic street near the harbor is lined with salty local tapas bars, with a few trendy ones mixed in (✪ see page 151).

The Eixample: Barcelona's upscale uptown is better for classy tapas in the evening than for after-midnight partying. For cocktail bars with breezy outdoor seating, try the parklike Rambla de Catalunya. A couple of blocks over, Carrer d'Enric Granados and Carrer d'Aribau draw the gay community.

Barceloneta: The broad beach is dotted with chiringuitos—shacks selling drinks and snacks, creating a fun, lively scene on a balmy summer evening. At the north end of the beach (in the former Olympic Village) are a number of trendy, exclusive, and expensive discos, including Opium Mar (www.opiummar.com). These places get going extremely late, and you must be "somebody" (or look good) to get in. I couldn't find a single place willing to check my rucksack.

Tours

Hop-On Hop-Off Bus Tours: Double-decker buses give tourists a drive-by look at major landmarks while listening to recorded descriptions. In Barcelona, I use these not merely as an overview of the city, but also as handy transportation to out-of-the-way sights.

Tourist Bus (Bus Turístic) offers two main routes, centered on their hub on Plaça de Catalunya. The two-hour blue route (departing from near El Corte Inglés) covers north Barcelona (most Gaudí sights). The two-hour red route (from the west side of the Plaça) covers south Barcelona (Barri Gòtic and Montjuïc). One-day (€27) and two-day (€38) tickets also come with 10-20 percent discounts off major sights and walking tours. Buy tickets on the bus, at the TI, or online. Tourist Bus operates daily 9:00-20:00 in summer, until 19:00 in winter (free Wi-Fi on board, www.barcelonabus turistic.cat). A different company, Barcelona City Tour, offers a nearly identical service (www.barcelonacitytour.cat).

Walking Tours: Several companies take groups of 10-30 people on two-hour guided walks in English, giving a once-over of Barcelona's history, culture, and sights for around €15-20. You just show up at the meeting point and pay your fee (though reserving ahead is always smart). The TI at Plaça de Sant Jaume offers great guided walks through the Barri Gòtic (daily at 9:30, reserve a day ahead in summer, tel. 932-853-832, www. barcelonaturisme.cat). The TI at Plaça de Catalunya offers a number of theme walks: Picasso, gourmet walks, Modernisme, and more.

Some companies offer "free" walks that rely on—and expect—a tip at the end. For these, I tip €5 minimum, and up to €15 for excellence. Try Runner Bean Tours (mobile 636-108-776, www.runnerbeantours.com) or Discover Walks (tel. 931-816-810, www.discoverwalks.com).

For around €200, you can hire your own private guide for a few hours. Try the Barcelona Guide Bureau (tel. 932-682-422, www.barcelonaguide bureau.com) or José Soler (mobile 615-059-326, www.pepitotours.com).

Guided Bus Tours: Several companies offer bus tours of Barcelona with an English-speaking guide for around €65. These can be handy for reaching outlying sights (such as Sagrada Família or Park Güell) or day-trip destinations (Montserrat or Figueres). Try the Barcelona Guide Bureau (tel. 933-152-261, www.barcelonaguidebureau.com) or Catalunya Tourist Bus (tel. 932-853-832, www.catalunyabusturistic.com).

Bike Tours: A fun way to see the city is with a group of other cyclists on rental bikes (around €20-25). Near Plaça Sant Jaume, try Barcelona by Bicycle (tel. 932-682-105, www.bicicletabarcelona.com).

RESOURCES FROM RICK STEVES

This Pocket guide is one of dozens of titles in my series of guidebooks on European travel. I also produce a public television series, *Rick Steves' Europe*, and a public radio show, *Travel with Rick Steves*. My website, www.ricksteves.com, offers a wealth of free travel resources, including videos and podcasts of my shows, audio tours of Europe's great sights, travel forums, guidebook updates, and information on European rail—plus an online travel store and specifics on our tours of Europe. If you want to be my virtual travel partner, follow me on Facebook and Twitter as I share my latest news and on-the-road spills, thrills, and insights. If you have feedback on this book, please fill out the survey at www.ricksteves. com/feedback. It helps us and fellow travelers.

Spanish Survival Phrases

In the phonetics, the italicized *h* sounds like the gutteral **j** in Baja California.

Good day.	**Buenos días.**	**bway**-nohs dee-ahs
Do you speak English?	**¿Habla Usted inglés?**	**ah**-blah oo-**stehd** een-**glays**
Yes. / No.	**Sí. / No.**	see / noh
I (don't) understand.	**(No) comprendo.**	(noh) kohm-**prehn**-doh
Please.	**Por favor.**	por fah-**bor**
Thank you.	**Gracias.**	**grah**-thee-ahs
I'm sorry.	**Lo siento.**	loh see-**ehn**-toh
Excuse me.	**Perdóneme.**	pehr-**doh**-nay-may
(No) problem.	**(No) problema.**	(noh) proh-**blay**-mah
Good.	**Bueno.**	**bway**-noh
Goodbye.	**Adiós.**	ah-dee-**ohs**
one / two	**uno / dos**	**oo**-noh / dohs
three / four	**tres / cuatro**	trays / **kwah**-troh
five / six	**cinco / seis**	**theen**-koh / says
seven / eight	**siete / ocho**	see-**eh**-tay / **oh**-choh
nine / ten	**nueve / diez**	**nway**-bay / dee-**ayth**
How much is it?	**¿Cuánto cuesta?**	**kwahn**-toh **kway**-stah
Write it?	**¿Me lo escribe?**	may loh ay-**skree**-bay
Is it free?	**¿Es gratis?**	ays **grah**-tees
Is it included?	**¿Está incluido?**	ay-**stah** een-kloo-**ee**-doh
Where can I buy / find...?	**¿Dónde puedo comprar / encontrar...?**	**dohn**-day **pway**-doh kohm-**prar** / ayn-kohn-**trar**
I'd like / We'd like...	**Quiero / Queremos...**	kee-**ehr**-oh / kehr-**ay**-mohs
...a room.	**...una habitación.**	**oo**-nah ah-bee-tah-thee-**ohn**
...a ticket to ___.	**...un billete para ___.**	oon bee-**yeh**-tay **pah**-rah ___
Where is...?	**¿Dónde está...?**	**dohn**-day ay-**stah**
...the train station	**...la estación de trenes**	lah ay-stah-thee-**ohn** day **tray**-nays
...the tourist information office	**...la oficina de turismo**	lah oh-fee-**thee**-nah day too-**rees**-moh
Where are the toilets?	**¿Dónde están los servicios?**	**dohn**-day ay-**stahn** lohs sehr-**bee**-thee-ohs
men	**hombres, caballeros**	**ohm**-brays, kah-bah-**yay**-rohs
women	**mujeres, damas**	moo-**heh**-rays, **dah**-mahs
left / right	**izquierda / derecha**	eeth-kee-**ehr**-dah / day-**ray**-chah
straight	**derecho**	day-**ray**-choh
When do you open / close?	**¿A qué hora abren / cierran?**	ah kay **oh**-rah **ah**-brehn / thee-**ay**-rahn
At what time?	**¿A qué hora?**	ah kay **oh**-rah
Just a moment.	**Un momento.**	oon moh-**mehn**-toh
now / soon / later	**ahora / pronto / más tarde**	ah-**oh**-rah / **prohn**-toh / mahs **tar**-day
today / tomorrow	**hoy / mañana**	oy / mahn-**yah**-nah

Practicalities

In a Spanish Restaurant

English	Spanish	Pronunciation
I'd like / We'd like...	Quiero / Queremos...	kee-**ehr**-oh / kehr-**ay**-mohs
...to reserve...	...reservar...	ray-sehr-**bar**
...a table for	...una mesa para	oo-nah **may**-sah **pah**-rah
one / two.	uno / dos.	**oo**-noh / dohs
Is this table free?	¿Está esta mesa libre?	ay-**stah** ay-stah **may**-sah **lee**-bray
The menu (in English), please.	La carta (en inglés), por favor.	lah **kar**-tah (ayn een-**glays**) por fah-**bor**
service (not) included	servicio (no) incluido	sehr-**bee**-thee-oh (noh) een-kloo-**ee**-doh
to go	para llevar	**pah**-rah yay-**bar**
with / without	con / sin	kohn / seen
and / or	y / o	ee / oh
fixed-price meal (of the day)	menú (del día)	may-**noo** (dayl **dee**-ah)
specialty of the house	especialidad de la casa	ay-spay-thee-ah-lee-**dahd** day lah **kah**-sah
combination plate	plato combinado	**plah**-toh kohm-bee-**nah**-doh
appetizers	tapas	**tah**-pahs
bread	pan	pahn
cheese	queso	**kay**-soh
sandwich	bocadillo	boh-kah-**dee**-yoh
soup	sopa	**soh**-pah
salad	ensalada	ayn-sah-**lah**-dah
meat	carne	**kar**-nay
poultry	aves	**ah**-bays
fish	pescado	pay-**skah**-doh
seafood	marisco	mah-**ree**-skoh
dessert	postres	**poh**-strays
tap water	agua del grifo	**ah**-gwah dayl **gree**-foh
mineral water	agua mineral	**ah**-gwah mee-nay-**rahl**
milk	leche	**lay**-chay
(orange) juice	zumo (de naranja)	**thoo**-moh (day nah-**rahn**-hah)
coffee / tea	café / té	kah-**feh** / tay
wine	vino	**bee**-noh
red / white	tinto / blanco	**teen**-toh / **blahn**-koh
glass / bottle	vaso / botella	**bah**-soh / boh-**tay**-yah
beer	cerveza	thehr-**bay**-thah
Cheers!	¡Salud!	sah-**lood**
More. / Another.	Más. / Otro.	mahs / **oh**-troh
The same.	El mismo.	ehl **mees**-moh
The bill, please.	La cuenta, por favor.	lah **kwayn**-tah por fah-**bor**
tip	propina	proh-**pee**-nah
Delicious!	¡Delicioso!	day-lee-thee-**oh**-soh

For many more phrases, check out *Rick Steves' Spanish Phrase Book*.

Catalan Survival Phrases

English	Catalan	Pronunciation
Hello.	Hola.	**oh**-lah
Do you speak English?	Parla anglès?	**par**-lah ahn-**glays**
Yes. / No.	Sí. / No.	see / noh
I (don't) understand.	(No) entenc.	(noh) ahn-**tehnk**
Please.	Si us plau.	see oos plow
Thank you (very much).	(Moltes) Gràcies.	(**mohl**-tahs) **grah**-see-ahs
I'm sorry.	Ho sento.	oo **sehn**-too
Excuse me.	Perdó.	pahr-**doh**
(No) problem.	(Cap) problema.	(kahp) pruh-**bleh**-mah
Good.	Bé.	bay
Goodbye.	Adéu.	ah-**day**-oo
one / two	un / dos	oon / dohs
three / four	tres / quatre	trehs / **kwah**-trah
five / six	cinc / sis	seenk / sees
seven / eight	set / vuit	seht / **voo**-eet
nine / ten	nou / deu	**noh**-oo / **deh**-oo
How much?	Quant és?	kwahn ehs
Write it?	M'ho escriu?	moh ah-**skree**-oo
Is it free?	És gratis?	ehs **grah**-tees
Is it included?	Està inclós?	ah-**stah** ihn-**klohs**
Where can I find / buy...?	On puc trobar / comprar...?	ohn pook troo-**bah** / koom-**prah**
I'd like...	Voldria...	vool-**dree**-ah
We'd like...	Voldríem...	vool-**dree**-ahm
...a room.	...una habitació	**oo**-nah ah-bee-tah-see-**oh**
...a ticket to ___.	...una entrada per ___.	**oo**-nah ahn-**trah**-dah pahr ___
Where is...?	On està...?	ohn ah-**stah**
...the train station	...l'estació del tren	lah-stah-see-**oh** dahl trehn
...the tourist information office	...l'oficina de turisme	loo-fee-**see**-nah dah too-**reez**-mah
...the toilet	...els serveis	ahls sahr-**vays**
men / women	homes / dones	**oh**-mahs / **doh**-nahs
left / right	esquerre / dreta	ahs-**keh**-reh / **dreh**-tah
straight	dret	dreht
At what time...?	A quina hora...?	ah **kee**-nah **oh**-rah
...does this open / close	...obre / tanca	**oh**-brah / **tahn**-kah
Just a moment.	Un moment.	oon moo-**mehn**
now / soon / later	ara / aviat / més tard	**ah**-rah / ah-vee-**aht** / mehs tahrd
today / tomorrow	avui / demà	ah-**vwee** / dah-**mah**
Long live Catalunya!	¡Visca Catalunya!	**vee**-skah kah-tah-**loon**-yah

Practicalities

In a Catalan Restaurant

English	Catalan	Pronunciation
I'd like to reserve...	**Voldria reservar...**	vool-**dree**-ah rah-sahr-**vah**
We'd like to reserve...	**Voldríem reservar...**	vool-**dree**-ahm rah-sahr-**vah**
...a table for one / two	**...una taula per una / dues**	oo-nah tow-lah pahr oo-nah / doo-**ehs**
Is this table free?	**Està lliure aquesta taula?**	ah-**stah** yoo-rah ah-**kwehs**-tah tow-lah
The menu (in English), please.	**La carta (en anglès), si us plau.**	lah **kar**-tah (ahn ahn-**glays**) see oos plow
service (not) included	**servei (no) inclós**	sahr-**vay**ee (noh) ihn-**klohs**
to go	**per emportar**	pahr ahm-por-**tah**
with / without	**amb / sense**	ahm / **sehn**-sah
and / or	**i / o**	ee / oh
tapas (small plates)	**tapes**	**tah**-pahs
fixed-price meal (of the day)	**menú (del dia)**	mah-**noo** (dahl **dee**-ah)
daily special	**plat del dia**	plaht dahl **dee**-ah
specialty of the house	**especialitat de la casa**	ah-spah-see-ah-lee-**taht** dah lah **kah**-zah
combination plate	**plat combinat**	plaht koom-bee-**naht**
appetizers	**entrants**	ahn-**trahns**
bread	**pà**	pah
cheese	**formatge**	foor-**mah**-jah
sandwich	**entrepà**	ahn-trah-**pah**
soup	**sopa**	**soh**-pah
salad	**amanida**	ah-mah-**nee**-dah
meat	**carn**	karn
poultry	**aviram**	ah-vee-**rahm**
fish	**peix**	paysh
seafood	**marisc**	mah-**reesk**
dessert	**postres**	**poh**-strahs
(tap) water	**aigua (de l'aixeta)**	**eye**-wah (dah lah-**shay**-tah)
mineral water	**aigua mineral**	**eye**-wah mee-nah-**rahl**
milk	**llet**	yeht
(orange) juice	**suc (de taronja)**	sook (dah tah-**rohn**-zhah)
coffee / tea	**cafè / te**	kah-**feh** / teh
wine	**vi**	vee
red / white	**negre / blanc**	**neh**-grah / blahnk
sweet / dry / semi-dry	**dolç / sec / semi-sec**	dohls / sehk / **seh**-mee sehk
glass / bottle	**copa / ampolla**	**koh**-pah / ahm-**poy**-yah
beer	**cervesa**	sahr-**veh**-zah
Cheers!	**Salut!**	sah-**looy**
More. / Another.	**Més. / Un altre.**	mehs / oon **ahl**-trah
The same.	**El mateix.**	ahl mah-**taysh**
the bill	**el compte**	ahl **kohmp**-tah
tip	**propina**	proo-**pee**-nah
Delicious!	**Boníssim!**	boo-**nee**-seem

INDEX

A

Accommodations: *See* Sleeping
After-hours neighborhoods: 175–176
Airbnb.com: 138
Airport: 162
Air travel, websites: 160
Altarpiece Museum (Cathedral of
    Barcelona): 62
Ambulance: 169
Amusement park: *See* Tibidabo
Antiques, shopping for: 173
Apartment rentals: 138
Aquarium: 33
Arrival in Barcelona: 162–163
Articket BCN Sightseeing Pass: 170–171
Art museums: CaixaForum, 12, 132;
    Catalan Art Museum, 12, 130–131;
    Frederic Marès Museum, 112–113;
    Fundació Antoni Tàpies, 90–91;
    Fundació Joan Miró, 13, 129.
    See also Picasso Museum
Art Nouveau: *See* Modernisme
ATMs: 161
Audio Europe, Rick Steves: 178
Augustus Roman Temple: 50, 113
AVE train: 160
Avinguda del Portal de l'Angel: 37;
    shopping, 174
Avinguda Diagonal: 91–92

B

Barcelona Card: 171
Barcelona Cathedral: *See* Cathedral
    of Barcelona
Barcelona City Hall: 48

Barcelona harborfront: 8, 32–33;
    beaches, 13, 119; boat cruises, 33, 112
Barcelona History Museum: 13, 51, 114
Barcelona Zoo: 118–119
Barceloneta: 33, 119, 176; eating, 151, 176
Barri Gòtic: 8, 35–51; eating, 150–151;
    map, 38–39; nightlife, 176; orienta-
    tion, 36; shopping, 173; sightseeing,
    112–114; walking tour, 37–51
Bars: 144–147, 176; listings, 149–153.
    See also Tapas
Basílica i Temple Expiatori de la Sagrada
    Família: *See* Sagrada Família
Beaches: Barcelona, 13, 119; Figueres,
    134; Sitges, 134
Beer: 148. *See also* Bars
Betlem Church: 23–24
Biking: 40, 168; guided tours, 177
Block of Discord: 13, 88–90, 120–122
Blue Period, of Picasso: 68–69
Boat travel: cruise ship ports, 163;
    golondrinas, 33, 112
Boqueria Market: 12, 24–27, 110, 149
Bullring Mall: 132
Buses (bus travel): 162, 168; map,
    166–167; Montjuïc, 125, 128; tours,
    176–177
Business hours: 164

C

Cable car, Montjuïc: 125, 128
Cabs: 162, 168
Cadaqués: 134
Cafés: 147; listings, 149–153
Café Granja Viader: 23–24, 149
Café Zürich: 20
CaixaForum: 12, 132, 175

Canaletes Fountain: 20
Carrefour: 22
Carrer de la Diputació: 83–84
Carrer de la Fruita: 46–47
Carrer de la Mercè: 176
Carrer de la Palla: 43, 173
Carrer de la Portaferrissa: 23, 173
Carrer del Bisbe: 43, 44, 47
Carrer del Bisbe Bridge: 47
Carrer de l'Esparteria: 116
Carrer del Malcuinat: 116
Carrer dels Arcs: 41
Carrer de Montcada: 115
Carrer de Pau Claris: 84
Carrer de Petritxol: 173
Carrer de Sant Domènec del Call: 46
Carrer de València: 87–89
Casa Amatller: 89, 120–121
Casa Batlló: 13, 88–89, 120
Casa de l'Ardiaca: 43–44
Casa de les Punxes: 91, 121
Casa Gispert: 116
Casa Lleó Morera: 13, 89–90, 121–122
Casa Milà: 12, 91, 122–123, 175
Castle of Montjuïc: 128
Catalan Art Museum: 12, 130–131
Catalan College of Architects: 42
Catalan restaurant phrases: 182
Catalan survival phrases: 181
Catalunya: cultural overview, 8–9
Cathedral of Barcelona: 13, 42–43,
    53–62, 112; map, 55; orientation, 13,
    54; the tour, 56–62
Cell (mobile) phones: 168–170
Centre Cultural La Casa Elizalde: 13,
    87–88
Chiringuitos: 119, 176
Chocolate Museum: 118

Christopher Columbus Monument:
    30–32, 111
Churches and cathedrals: Betlem
    Church, 23–24; Holy Conception
    Church, 84; Santa Anna Church,
    37, 40; Santa Maria del Mar Church,
    13, 116, 118; Santa Maria del Pi
    Church, 27, 173, 175; Sant Felip Neri
    Church, 44–45. See also Cathedral
    of Barcelona; Sagrada Família
Citadel Park: 118–119
Ciutat Vella: See Old City
Climate: 160
Clothing sizes: 172–173
Columbus (Christopher) Monument:
    30–32, 111
Communicating: 168–170
Concepció Market: 84, 86
Consulates: 169
Credit cards: 161
Cruises: 33, 112
Cruise ship ports: 163
Cuban cigars: 24
Cubism: 71, 74
Cuisine: 147–148. See also Eating
Currency and exchange: 161
Customs regulations: 173

D
Daily reminder: 10–11
Dalí, Salvador: 41, 86, 134; House
    (Cadaqués), 134; Theater-Museum
    (Figueres), 134
Dance: flamenco, 175; sardana, 13, 112
Debit cards: 161
Discounts: 171
Domènech i Montaner, Lluís: 43–44,
    86–87, 89–90, 91–92, 117, 121–122

Drassanes Metro: 30, 165

E

Eating: 143–157; Catalan restaurant phrases, 182; cuisine, 147–148; eating on Spanish schedule, 144; listings, 149–153; maps, 154–157; price code, 144; Spanish restaurant phrases, 180; survival tips, 147; tipping, 161. *See also* Markets; Tapas

Eixample: 8, 77–92; background, 78–80; eating, 152–153; maps, 82, 156–157; nightlife, 176; orientation, 78; shopping, 174; sightseeing, 119–123; sleeping, 141; walking tour, 81–92

El Born: 8, 43; eating, 151–152; map, 115; nightlife, 176; shopping, 174; walking tour, 114–119

El Born Cultural Center: 116

El Call: *See* Jewish Quarter

El Corte Inglés: 20, 37, 145–146, 174

Electricity: 164

El Prat de Llobregat Airport: 162

Els Quatre Gats: 40, 68, 150

Email: 136, 169

Emergencies: 172

Entertainment: *See* Dance; Music

Escribà: 27

Espadrilles: 172

Estadi Olímpic: 130

Eulàlia, Saint: 60, 112

Euro currency: 161

F

Figueres: 134

Flamenco: 175

Font Màgica: 13, 131

Food: *See* Eating; Groceries; Markets; Tapas

Frederic Marès Museum: 112–113

Fundació Antoni Tàpies: 90–91

Fundació Joan Miró: 13, 129

Funicular, Montjuïc: 125, 128

G

Gaudí, Antoni: 86, 119, 121; Casa Batlló, 13, 88–89, 120; Casa Milà, 12, 91, 122–123, 175; House Museum, 125; Palau Güell, 12, 29–30, 110; Park Güell, 12, 123–125; tomb, 105. *See also* Sagrada Família

Gay men and lesbians: 79, 134, 176

Gimeno: 24

Golondrinas: 33, 112

Gothic Quarter: *See* Barri Gòtic

Gràcia: 8, 91–92

Gran Teatre del Liceu: 28, 175

Graus Olives i Conserves: 26

Groceries: 146. *See also* Markets

Güell, Eusebi: 87, 123

Güell Palace (Palau Güell): 12, 29–30, 110

Güell Park: 12, 123–125; map, 124

Guided tours: 176–177

H

Harborfront: *See* Barcelona harborfront

Holidays: 164

Holy Conception Church: 84

Holy Family Church: *See* Sagrada Família

Horta de San Joan: 67–68

Hotel Casa Fuster: 91–92, 121, 175

Hotels: *See* Sleeping

I

Illa de la Discòrdia: *See* Block of Discord

Information: *See* Tourist information
Internet access: 136, 169
Itineraries: 10–11, 14

J

Jamboree: 175
Jazz music: 92, 175, 176
Jewish Quarter: 46
J. Murria Queviures: 87
Joan Miró Foundation: 13, 129
Jujol, Josep Maria: 87, 124

L

La Boqueria Market: *See* Boqueria Market
La Concepció Market: 84, 86
La Mercè: 58
Language: Catalan restaurant phrases, 182; Catalan survival phrases, 181; Spanish restaurant phrases, 180; Spanish survival phrases, 179
Language barrier: 163
La Pedrera (Casa Milà): 12, 91, 122–123, 175
La Rambla: *See* Ramblas
La Rambla de Mar: 33
La Ribera: *See* El Born
La Sagrada Família: *See* Sagrada Família
Las Arenas: 132
Laundry: 164
Liceu Metro: 27, 165
Liceu Opera House: 28, 175
Live music: 174–175

M

Magic Fountains: 13, 131
Maps: Barcelona excursions, 133; Barri

Gòtic, 38–39; Cathedral of Barcelona, 55; eating, 154–157; Eixample, 82, 156–157; El Born, 115; Montjuïc, 126–127; neighborhoods, 7; Old City, 108–109, 154–155; Park Güell, 124; Picasso Museum, 65; public transportation, 166–167; Ramblas, 18–19; Sagrada Família, 97
Marès (Frederic) Museum: 112–113
Maritime Museum: 12–13, 111
Markets: La Concepció, 84, 86; Santa Caterina, 13, 43, 115, 117. *See also* Boqueria Market
Medical help: 172
Metric system: 164
Metro: 165; to/from airport, 162–163; map, 166–167
Mies van der Rohe Pavilion: 132
Miró, Joan: 27; Foundation, 13, 129
Mobile phones: 168–170
Modernisme: 80, 86–87, 121. *See also* Domènech i Montaner, Lluís; Gaudí, Antoni; Puig i Cadafalch, Josep
Moll Adossat: 163
Money: 161
Money belts: 161, 172
Montjuïc: 8, 33, 125–132; map, 126–127; transportation, 125, 128
Montjuïc Castle: 128
Montserrat: 133–134
Monument a Colóm: 30–32, 111
Monument of Catalan Independence: 116
Monument to the Martyrs of Independence: 44
Museu Capitular (Cathedral of Barcelona): 62
Museu de la Xocolata: 118
Museu del Calçat: 46, 113

Museu d'Història de Barcelona: Plaça del Rei: 13, 51, 114

Museu Marítim: 12–13, 111

Museu Nacional d'Art de Catalunya: 12, 130–131

Museu Olímpic i de l'Esport: 130

Museu Picasso: *See* Picasso Museum

Music: 174–175

N

Neighborhoods: 7–8; after-hours, 175–176; map, 7. *See also specific neighborhoods*

Nightlife: 174–176

O

Ocaña: 29

Old City: 8; eating, 149–151; maps, 108–109, 154–155; sightseeing, 110–119; sleeping, 139–140. *See also* Barri Gòtic; El Born; Jewish Quarter; Ramblas

Old Main Synagogue: 36, 46

Old Port: 33

Olympic and Sports Museum: 130

Olympic Stadium: 130

ONCE booths: 22

Organized tours: 176–177

P

Palace of Catalan Music: 12, 117, 174–175

Palau Baró de Quadras: 91, 121

Palau de la Generalitat: 48

Palau de la Música Catalana: 12, 117, 174–175

Palau Güell: 12, 29–30, 110

Palau Reial Major: 50–51

Parc de la Ciutadella: 118–119

Park Güell: 12, 123–125; map, 124

Passatge Permanyer: 84

Passeig de Gràcia: 17, 79, 81, 83; shopping, 174

Passeig del Born: 115–116

Passports: 160, 172

Pharmacies: 172

Phone numbers, useful: 169

Phones: 169–170

Picasso, Pablo: 42; biographical sketch, 70–72. *See also* Picasso Museum

Picasso Museum: 63–75, 117; eating near, 151–152; map, 65; orientation, 12, 64; the tour, 66–75

Pinotxo Bar: 25, 149

Plaça d'Antoni Maura: 115

Plaça de Catalunya: 8, 17, 20, 37; shopping, 174; sleeping, 139; tourist information, 163

Plaça del Rei: 50–51

Plaça de Sant Jaume: 47–48

Plaça d'Espanya: 13, 131

Plaça Nova: 41–42

Plaça Reial: 12, 29–30, 110–111; nightlife, 176

Plaça Sant Felip Neri: 44, 46, 47–48

Planelles Donat: 37

Planning tips: 10–11, 14, 160

Poble Espanyol: 13, 132

Police: 169

Puig i Cadafalch, Josep: 40, 87, 89, 91, 120–121, 132

Q

Quadrat d'Or: 79

R

Rail travel: *See* Train travel

Rambla de Catalunya: 90–91
Rambla of Flowers: 24
Rambla of the Little Birds: 22–23
Ramblas: 8, 15–34, 110; eating, 149; map, 18–19; orientation, 12, 16; sightseeing, 110–114; sleeping, 139–140; walking tour, 17–34
Raval: 8, 30
Reader feedback: 178
Reial Cercle Artistic Museum: 41
Renaixença: 80, 83
Rental properties: 138
Resources from Rick Steves: 178
Restaurants: 144–146; Catalan phrases, 182; listings, 149–153; Spanish phrases, 180; tipping, 161
Restrooms: 164
Ribera: See El Born
Roman sites (ancient Romans): 35, 41–42, 46, 48, 56, 114; aqueduct, 42; necropolis, 23; Temple of Augustus, 50, 113
Rose Period, of Picasso: 69, 73
Royal Academy of Science: 22
Royal Palace: 50–51

S

Sabater Hermanos: 46
Safety: 171–172
Sagrada Família: 93–105, 123; background, 95; map, 97; orientation, 12, 94; the tour, 96–105
Saint Agatha Chapel: 51
Santa Anna Church: 37, 40
Santa Caterina Market: 13, 43, 115, 117
Santa Eulàlia (schooner): 111
Santa Maria del Mar Church: 13, 116, 118
Santa Maria del Pi Church: 27, 173, 175

Sant Felip Neri Church: 44–45
Sants Train Station: 162–163
Sardana dances: 13, 112
Seasons: 160
Severus, Saint: 57
Shoe Museum: 46, 113
Shopping: 172–174; hours, 164; neighborhoods, 173–174
Sightseeing (sights): 107–134; at a glance, 12–13; daily reminder, 10–11; general tips, 170–171; itineraries, 10–11, 14; passes, 170–171; reservations, 170. See also specific sights
Sitges: 134
Sleeping: 135–141; budget tips, 137–138; listings, 139–141; price code, 136; reservations, 137; typical Barcelona hotel, 136–137
Smartphones: 168–170
Souvenir items: 172
Spanish restaurant phrases: 180
Spanish survival phrases: 179
Spanish Village: 13, 132
Sports Museum: 130
Subway: See Metro
Synagogue: 36, 46

T

Tapas: 146–147, 175–176; Eixample, 83–84, 153; listings, 149–153; maps, 154–157
Tapas 24: 83–84, 153
Tàpies (Antoni) Foundation: 90–91
Taverna Basca Irati: 28, 149
Taxes, VAT refunds: 173
Taxis: 162, 168
Teatre del Liceu: 28, 175
Telephone numbers, useful: 169

Telephones: 169–170
Temple of Augustus: 50, 113
Theft: 171–172
Tibidabo: 125
Tickets: 174
Time Out BCN Guide: 174
Time zone: 164
Tipping: 161
Toilets: 164
Tourist information: 160, 163
Tours: 176–177
Train travel: 162–163; websites: 160
Transportation: to Barcelona, 162–163;
    within Barcelona, 165–168; map,
    166–167
Travel insurance: 160
Travel websites: 160

V
VAT refunds: 173
Velázquez, Diego: 74

Viceroy's Palace: 51
Vinçon: 91, 174
Visitor information: *See* Tourist
    information

W
Walking tours: Barri Gòtic, 37–51;
    Eixample, 81–92; El Born, 114–119;
    guided, 177; Ramblas, 17–34
Water Tower Garden: 84
Weather: 160
Websites: 160
Wine: 148
World Expo Fairgrounds: 13, 131

Z
Zoen: 46
Zoo de Barcelona: 118–119

Index

Explore Europe

At ricksteves.com you can browse through thousands of articles, videos, photos and radio interviews, plus find a wealth of money-saving travel tips for planning your dream trip. And with our mobile-friendly website, you can easily access all this great travel information anywhere you go.

TV Shows

Preview the places you'll visit by watching entire half-hour episodes of Rick Steves' Europe (choose from all 100 shows) on-demand, for free.

ricksteves.com

your travel dreams into affordable reality

Radio Interviews

Enjoy ready access to Rick's vast library of radio interviews covering

travel tips and cultural insights that relate specifically to your Europe travel plans.

Travel Forums

Learn, ask, share! Our online community of savvy travelers is a great resource for first-time travelers to Europe, as well as seasoned pros. You'll find forums on each country, plus travel tips and restaurant/hotel reviews. You can even ask one of our well-traveled staff to chime in with an opinion.

Travel News

Subscribe to our free Travel News e-newsletter, and get monthly updates from Rick on what's happening in Europe.

Audio Europe™

Rick's Free Travel App

Get your FREE Rick Steves Audio Europe™ app to enjoy…

- Dozens of self-guided tours of Europe's top museums, sights and historic walks
- Hundreds of tracks filled with cultural insights and sightseeing tips from Rick's radio interviews
- All organized into handy geographic playlists
- For iPhone, iPad, iPod Touch, Android

With Rick whispering in your ear, Europe gets even better.

Find out more at ricksteves.com

Pack Light and Right

Gear up for your next adventure at ricksteves.com

Light Luggage

Pack light and right with Rick Steves' affordable, custom-designed rolling carry-on bags, backpacks, day packs and shoulder bags.

Accessories

From packing cubes to moneybelts and beyond, Rick has personally selected the travel goodies that will help your trip go smoother.

Shop at ricksteves.com

Rick Steves has

Save time and energy

This guidebook is your independent-travel toolkit. But for all it delivers, it's still up to you to devote the time and energy it takes to manage the preparation and logistics that are essential for a happy trip. If that's a hassle, there's a solution.

Rick Steves Tours

A Rick Steves tour takes you to Europe's most interesting places with great guides and small groups

great tours, too!

with minimum stress

of 28 or less. We follow Rick's favorite itineraries, ride in comfy buses, stay in family-run hotels, and bring you intimately close to the Europe you've traveled so far to see. Most importantly, we take away the logistical headaches so you can focus on the fun.

Join the fun
This year we'll take 18,000 free-spirited travelers—nearly half of them repeat customers—along with us on 40 different itineraries, from Ireland to Italy to Istanbul. Is a Rick Steves tour the right fit for your travel dreams? Find out at ricksteves.com, where you can also get Rick's latest tour catalog and free Tour Experience DVD.

Europe is best experienced with happy travel partners. We hope you can join us.

See our itineraries at ricksteves.com

Rick Steves®

BEST OF GUIDES

Best of France
Best of Germany
Best of Ireland
Best of Italy
Best of Spain

EUROPE GUIDES

Best of Europe
Eastern Europe
Europe Through the Back Door
Mediterranean Cruise Ports
Northern European Cruise Ports

COUNTRY GUIDES

Croatia & Slovenia
England
France
Germany
Great Britain
Ireland
Italy
Portugal
Scandinavia
Scotland
Spain
Switzerland

CITY & REGIONAL GUIDES

Amsterdam & the Netherlands
Belgium: Bruges, Brussels, Antwerp & Ghent
Barcelona
Budapest
Florence & Tuscany
Greece: Athens & the Peloponnese
Istanbul
London
Paris
Prague & the Czech Republic
Provence & the French Riviera
Rome
Venice
Vienna, Salzburg & Tirol

SNAPSHOT GUIDES

Basque Country: Spain & France
Berlin
Copenhagen & the Best of Denmark
Dublin
Dubrovnik
Hill Towns of Central Italy
Italy's Cinque Terre
Krakow, Warsaw & Gdansk
Lisbon
Loire Valley

Nearly all Rick Steves guides are available as ebooks. Check with your favorite bookseller.
Rick Steves guidebooks are published by Avalon Travel, a member of the Perseus Books Group.

Maximize your travel skills with a good guidebook.

Madrid & Toledo
Milan & the Italian Lakes District
Naples & the Amalfi Coast
Northern Ireland
Norway
Sevilla, Granada & Southern Spain
St. Petersburg, Helsinki & Tallinn
Stockholm

POCKET GUIDES
Amsterdam
Athens
Barcelona
Florence
London
Munich & Salzburg
Paris
Prague
Rome
Venice
Vienna

TRAVEL CULTURE
Europe 101
European Christmas
Postcards from Europe
Travel as a Political Act

***RICK STEVES' EUROPE* DVDs**
12 New Shows 2015–2016
Austria & the Alps
The Complete Collection 2000-2016
Eastern Europe

England & Wales
European Christmas
European Travel Skills & Specials
France
Germany, BeNeLux & More
Greece, Turkey & Portugal
The Holy Land: Israelis & Palestinians Today
Iran
Ireland & Scotland
Italy's Cities
Italy's Countryside
Scandinavia
Spain
Travel Extras

PHRASE BOOKS & DICTIONARIES
French
French, Italian & German
German
Italian
Portuguese
Spanish

PLANNING MAPS
Britain, Ireland & London
Europe
France & Paris
Germany, Austria & Switzerland
Ireland
Italy
Spain & Portugal

RickSteves.com 🅕 🅣 @RickSteves

Rick Steves books are available at bookstores and through online booksellers.

Photo © Patricia Feaster

PHOTO CREDITS

Other photos © David C. Hoerlein

Eixample Walk

© Cameron Hewitt, Suzanne Kotz, Robyn Stencil; additional images from Wikimedia Commons

Sagrada Família Tour

© Cameron Hewitt, Rick Steves

Sights

© Cameron Hewitt, Rick Steves, Robyn Stencil; additional images from Wikimedia Commons

Sleeping

© Robyn Stencil, Dominic Bonuccelli

Eating

© Suzanne Kotz, Rick Steves

Practicalities

© Cameron Hewitt, Rick Steves

to Mercat Fira de Bellcaire (Els Encants)
left to Girona, rt Plaça de Tetuan, slight left
    onto Gran Via de les Corts Catalanes,
    rt out los Castillejos, on left.

Glories ◇M◇ right near Els Encants

---

from Glories L1 to Pl. Espanya
    take exit Tarragona
walk 40m to
    Pl Espanya-Centre
    Commercial Las Arenas
    [150]   Av Miramar - Fundacio Joan Miro

---

back → walking - 48 min

Avalon Travel
a member of the Perseus Books Group
1700 Fourth Street
Berkeley, CA 94710, USA

ISBN 978-1-63121-311-3
ISSN 2326-1994

For the latest on Rick's lectures, books, tours, public-radio show, and public-television
series, contact Rick Steves' Europe, 130 Fourth Avenue North, Edmonds, WA 98020,
tel. 425/771-8303, www.ricksteves.com, rick@ricksteves.com.

Rick Steves' Europe
Special Publications Manager: Risa Laib
Managing Editor: Jennifer Madison Davis
Editors: Glenn Eriksen, Tom Griffin, Suzanne Kotz, Cathy Lu, Carrie Shepherd
Editorial & Production Assistant: Jessica Shaw
Researcher: Amanda Buttinger
Maps & Graphics: Barb Geisler, David C. Hoerlein, Sandra Hundacker, Lauren Mills,
Mary Rostad

Avalon Travel
Senior Editor and Series Manager: Madhu Prasher
Editor: Jamie Andrade
Associate Editors: Sierra Machado, Maggie Ryan
Copy Editor: Kelly Lydick
Proofreader: Rebecca Freed
Indexer: Stephen Callahan
Production & Typesetting: McGuire Barber Design, Tabitha Lahr
Cover Design: Kimberly Glyder Design
Maps & Graphics: Kat Bennett, Mike Morgenfeld

ABOUT THE AUTHORS

Rick Steves

Rick writes a best-selling guidebook series; produces a public television series *(Rick Steves' Europe)*, public radio show *(Travel with Rick Steves)*, a blog (on Facebook), and an app and podcast *(Rick Steves Audio Europe)*; and organizes guided tours that take over 20,000 travelers to Europe annually. Rick's mission is to make European travel fun, affordable, and culturally enlightening for Americans.

Connect with Rick: facebook.com/RickSteves 🐦 twitter: @RickSteves

Gene Openshaw

Gene has co-authored a dozen *Rick Steves* books, specializing in walking tours of Europe's cultural sights. He also contributes to Rick's public television series, produces tours for *Rick Steves Audio Europe,* and is a regular guest on Rick's public radio show. He lives near Seattle with his daughter and roots for the Mariners in good times and bad.

Cameron Hewitt

Cameron writes guidebooks and serves as content manager for Rick Steves' Europe. For this book, he gorged on Gaudí, bored into El Born, marveled at Miró, aced the Eixample, and sashayed the *sardana* in front of the cathedral. When he's not traveling, Cameron lives in Seattle with his wife Shawna.

FOLDOUT COLOR MAP

The foldout map on the opposite page includes:

• Maps of Barcelona on one side

• Maps of Barcelona and Spain on the other side